LOWELL: A Study of Industrial Development

KENNIKAT PRESS SCHOLARLY REPRINTS

Dr. Ralph Adams Brown, Senior Editor

Series on
MAN AND HIS ENVIRONMENT
Under the General Editorial Supervision of
Dr. Roger C. Heppell
Professor of Geography, State University of New York

LOWELL

A Study of Industrial Development

by Margaret Terrell Parker

KENNIKAT PRESS
Port Washington, N. Y./London

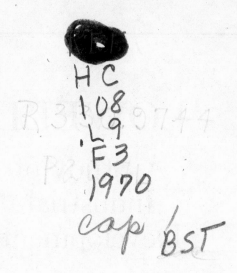
LOWELL: A STUDY OF INDUSTRIAL DEVELOPMENT

First published in 1940
Reissued in 1970 by Kennikat Press
Library of Congress Catalog Card No: 73-118421
ISBN 0-8046-1373-7

Manufactured by Taylor Publishing Company   Dallas, Texas

KENNIKAT SERIES ON MAN AND HIS ENVIRONMENT

FOREWORD

THIS STUDY was undertaken at the suggestion
of Professor Harlan H. Barrows, Chairman of the
Department of Geography of the University of
Chicago. The manuscript was submitted to the
Faculty of the Division of Physical Sciences of the
University of Chicago in partial fulfillment of the
requirements for the degree of Doctor of Philoso-
phy. It represents a portion of an investigation
which has been in progress for several years while
the author has been a member of the Faculty of
Wellesley College, and which has been concerned
with other cities of the lower Merrimack Valley as
well as with Lowell.

The field work in Lowell which provided data for
the maps and text of the book was completed in the
spring of 1938. Since the details of the industrial
pattern change rapidly, it is inevitable that minor
changes in the number and location of industrial
establishments will have occurred during the interval
in which the material was being prepared for publication.

The author makes grateful acknowledgment to
Mr. Barrows for valuable suggestions and critical
examination of the text, and to Mr. Henry M.
Leppard for helpful advice concerning maps. She
expresses sincere thanks to many residents of
Lowell, without whose cooperation the study would

v

have been impossible. To all manufacturers who so
generously gave their time to supplying oral or
written information, and to others who were helpful
in a variety of ways, the author is deeply grateful.

MARGARET TERRELL PARKER

TABLE OF CONTENTS

An Industrial City
Evidences of Change
The Present Industrial Pattern
The Commercial Districts

The Central Industrial Area
The Early Commercial Center
An Early Civic Center
Early Distribution of Settlement
The Concord Industrial Area
The Railroads and the Railroad Industrial Areas
Expansion of the Residential Districts
The Street Pattern
Other Features of the Pattern
Recent Changes in the Industrial Pattern

Power
Water for Processing

LIST OF TABLES

ix

LIST OF MAPS

LIST OF FIGURES

xi

LOWELL: A Study of Industrial Development

CHAPTER 1

An Old City and a Modern Problem

LOWELL, Massachusetts, long known as "The Spindle City" and "The Queen City of the Merrimack" (Map I), completed in 1936 a century of life as an industrial city. The origin and growth of Lowell constitute the first instance in America of the development of a city of the primarily industrial type, a city which owes its existence to its mills. There are in New England other manufacturing cities whose first mills were established earlier than those of Lowell; Pawtucket, Rhode Island, is a notable example. But the spectacular early growth of Lowell brought it to urban dimensions and resultant city status years before Pawtucket or any other mill town attained that status. No other American community of industrial origin has been a city for so long as one hundred years.

During this century of industrial cityhood which Lowell has recently completed, the city's history for more than eight decades was, on the whole, one of growth—of expanding industries and increasing population. There were in the course of these years some reverses and, in the expansion of industries, some periods of quiescence between periods of growth, but the general trend was upward, and in 1918 Lowell's manufactures, stimulated by war demand, reached levels well above those attained in any previous year.[1]

Since that year the city's industries have experienced not only the immediate decreases to be expected with the cessation of war production but a further serious decline. The latter years of the century were years of difficulty, of changing industries, and loss of population. Manufacturing in Lowell employed approximately forty thousand workers in 1918,[2] thirty thousand in 1919,[3] and between fifteen and sixteen thousand in 1936.[4] The year 1936 was one of relative prosperity as compared with those immediately preceding it. Complete data since 1936 are not available. The business recession which began in the latter half of 1937 has again reduced employment. Totals prepared by the Chamber of Commerce of numbers employed in one hundred establishments in the first two months of 1938 are 22 per cent lower than corresponding figures for 1936. In total value of manufactured products

[1] Commonwealth of Massachusetts, Bureau of Statistics, *Annual Reports on the Statistics of Manufactures.* (Issued before 1909 by Bureau of Statistics of Labor; 1919–21 by Department of Labor and Industries.)

[2] *Ibid.,* 1918, p. 22.

[3] *Ibid.,* 1919, p. 23.

[4] Commonwealth of Massachusetts, Department of Labor and Industries, Division of Statistics, "Census of Manufactures, 1936, City of Lowell, Massachusetts" (Mfrs., 1936: No. 17, mimeographed), p. 1.

MAP I

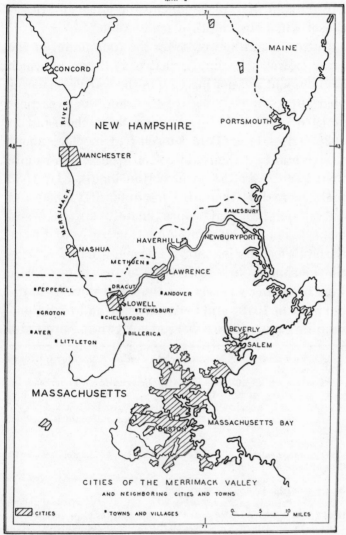

CITIES OF THE MERRIMACK VALLEY
AND NEIGHBORING CITIES AND TOWNS

Lowell held fifth place among the cities of Massachusetts in 1918,[1] ninth place in 1936.[2]

Cotton manufacture, from the foundation of the town Lowell's leading industry, and one in which employment did not increase in the war years, occupied approximately twelve thousand wage earners in 1918 [3] and 1919 [4]—less than three thousand in 1936.[5] As late as 1925 Lowell had in place about twelve hundred thousand cotton spindles and more than twenty-six thousand cotton looms.[6] In 1936 there were less than two hundred fifty thousand active spindles and approximately six thousand looms.[7] The manufacture of cotton has ceased to be the city's leading industry. The manufacture of textile machinery has suffered a similar loss. There were between two and three thousand workers in the industry in 1919 [8] and between three and four thousand in 1920.[9] There were about two hundred and

---

[1] Commonwealth of Massachusetts, *Statistics of Manufactures, 1918,* p. xxxiv.

[2] Commonwealth of Massachusetts, Department of Labor and Industries, Division of Statistics, "Census of Manufactures, 1936, Cities in Massachusetts" (Mfrs., 1936: No. 40, mimeographed), p. 2.

[3] Commonwealth of Massachusetts, *Statistics of Manufactures, 1918,* p. 22.

[4] *Ibid.,* 1919, p. 23.

[5] Commonwealth of Massachusetts, "Census of Manufactures, 1936, City of Lowell," p. 1.

[6] Totals calculated from figures in *American Wool and Cotton Reporter,* July 23, 1925, pp. 228–35.

[7] *Official American Textile Directory, 1937, Textile World* Publications (New York: McGraw-Hill Publishing Co., Inc.), pp. 140–41.

[8] Commonwealth of Massachusetts, *Statistics of Manufactures, 1919,* p. 24.

[9] *Ibid.,* 1920, p. 25.

fifty in 1936.[1] Other industries related to these two have followed in their wake. In contrast, the manufacture of woolen and worsted goods, which in 1918 ranked second among the city's industries in value of products and third in numbers employed,[2] maintained its importance. In 1936 it slightly exceeded in numbers employed and almost equaled in value of products the levels of 1918 and had become the city's leading manufacture.[3] Certain lesser manufactures have shown growth during the period in which the cotton and machinery industries have declined so sharply, but their growth has fallen far short of balancing the losses.

A decrease of population was a natural consequence. From 112,759 at the census of 1920 it dropped to 100,114 in 1935.[4] It is estimated, moreover, that 40 per cent of the present population receive financial aid in some form from the city, state, or federal government.[5] Considerable blocks of vacant industrial or residential property have been destroyed to reduce taxes. The city's heavy relief burdens and the demolition of property contribute to the mounting of tax rates, and industries struggle

---

[1] Commonwealth of Massachusetts, "Census of Manufactures, 1936, City of Lowell," p. 1.

[2] Commonwealth of Massachusetts, *Statistics of Manufactures, 1918,* p. 23.

[3] Commonwealth of Massachusetts, "Census of Manufactures, 1936, City of Lowell," p. 1.

[4] Commonwealth of Massachusetts, *The Decennial Census, 1935,* p. 13.

[5] Information supplied by Lowell Taxpayers Association.

with an increasing tax load while real estate to alarming degrees accrues to the city in payment of taxes or to the banks in cancellation of mortgages.

Thus the city which, a century ago, as a model manufacturing community and a daring experiment in industrial management, attracted the interest of students of social and economic questions throughout the United States and Europe begins the second century of its life faced by grave problems; their solution may require even more foresight, initiative, and energy than contributed to make Lowell America's first industrial city and for many years its leading center of cotton manufacture.

The economic vicissitudes through which Lowell has passed in the last two decades raise questions as to the imprints which the catastrophes of later years as well as the long preceding periods of industrial growth have left upon the city, the natural foundations upon which previous prosperity was based, and the reasons for recent changes. It is the function of this study to portray the city as it is today, to analyze the environmental factors involved in its evolution to its present status, and to consider problems which its future development presents.

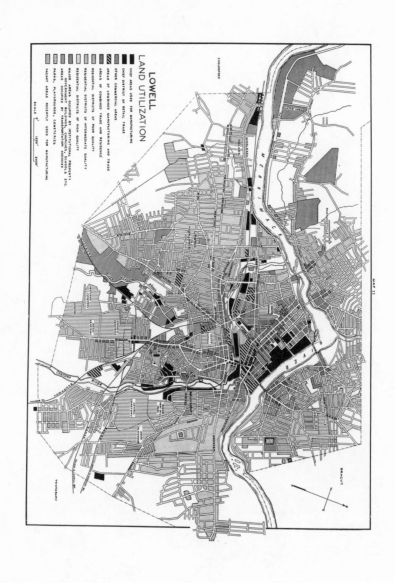

LOWELL
LAND UTILIZATION

CHIEF AREAS USED FOR MANUFACTURING
CHIEF DISTRICT OF RETAIL TRADE
OTHER COMMERCIAL AREAS
AREAS OF COMBINED MANUFACTURING AND RESIDENCE
AREAS OF COMBINED TRADE AND RESIDENCE
RESIDENTIAL DISTRICTS OF POOR QUALITY
RESIDENTIAL DISTRICTS OF INTERMEDIATE QUALITY
RESIDENTIAL DISTRICTS OF HIGH QUALITY
MAJOR AREAS OCCUPIED BY INSTITUTIONAL PROPERTY
GOVERNMENT BUILDINGS, CHURCHES, SCHOOLS & ETC.
AREAS OCCUPIED BY TRANSPORTATION AGENCIES
PARKS, PLAYGROUNDS, CEMETERIES
VACANT AREAS RECENTLY USED FOR MANUFACTURING

SCALE

MAP II

CHAPTER 2

Lowell Today

An Industrial City

MORE THAN a century of industry has left upon Lowell an indelible impression. The most casual observer could scarcely escape the conclusion that it is a mill city. The chief business district lies within a

FIG. 1. LOOKING FROM MERRIMACK STREET NORTHWARD ALONG THE MERRIMACK CANAL, DUTTON STREET, TOWARD THE MILLS OF THE MERRIMACK MANUFACTURING COMPANY.

7

FIG. 2. MILLS LINING THE SOUTH BANK OF THE MERRIMACK
EAST OF BRIDGE STREET; JUNCTION OF THE CONCORD AND MERRI-
MACK RIVERS AT THE LEFT; CENTRAL BRIDGE (BRIDGE STREET)
AT THE EXTREME RIGHT.

FIG. 3. MILLS LINING THE SOUTH BANK

8

belt of factories which almost encircles it (Map II).
Dignified, substantial structures of red brick, taller
than other buildings near them, the factories of this
central ring dominate the heart of the city. Looking
from Merrimack Street southward along Shattuck
(Map III) or northward along the various streets
between Bridge and Aiken (Map II), one sees each
one end against the solid red wall of the mills
(Fig. 1). Mill buildings border Jackson Street
(Map II) for almost the whole of its length. Entering the city from the north and crossing the Merrimack at Bridge Street (Map II), one is confronted
by the long rampart of factories which, unbroken
save by Bridge Street itself, lines the south bank of
the river from its junction with the Concord for
nearly a mile upstream (Figs. 2 and 3).

The Concord as well as the Merrimack is a focus
of industry. From the bridge over the Concord at

OF THE MERRIMACK WEST OF BRIDGE STREET.

Rogers Street there is visible, upstream, the cluster
of mills just north of the Lawrence Street crossing,
and, downstream, the belt of industrial plants which
flanks the right bank of the lower river (Map II and
Fig. 4). A passenger crossing Lowell by train sees
neither these Concord mills nor those along the Merrimack but passes a long series of factories scattered
along the railroad from near the southern border of
the city to its western margin (Map II and Fig. 5).
There are few parts of Lowell where the mills can
be wholly forgotten; from the grassy summit of
Rogers Fort Hill Park (Map II and Fig. 6), the
city's chief pleasure ground, one looks down upon
the tanneries of the American Hide and Leather
Company spread along the western base of the hill
(Map II) and sees in the distance the smokestacks
which rise from the mills along the lower Concord
and the Merrimack.

In addition to the mills themselves, other signs
suggest the city's industrial importance—the dam
across the Merrimack visible from the School Street
bridge (Map II and Fig. 7), the stretch of foaming
rapids to be seen, at the season of high water, below
the dam, the several canals which intersect the heart
of the city (Map II), the railway tracks which cut
through the central business area to penetrate the
mill districts (Map III), the blocks of substantial
brick tenements and lodginghouses near the mills,
built by the textile corporations (Fig. 8). The im-
pressive plant of the Lowell Textile School (on

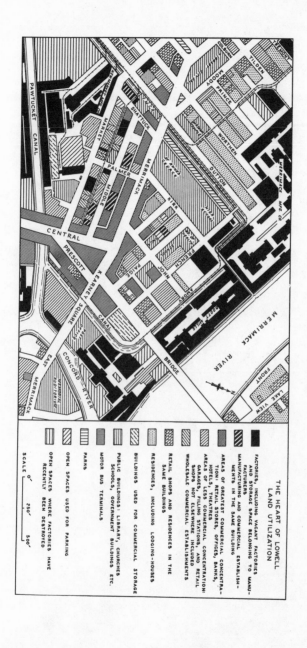

THE HEART OF LOWELL
LAND UTILIZATION

FACTORIES, INCLUDING VACANT FACTORIES
AND STORAGE SPACE BELONGING TO MANU-
FACTURERS

MANUFACTURING AND COMMERCIAL ESTABLISH-
MENTS IN THE SAME BUILDING

AREAS OF GREATEST COMMERCIAL CONCENTRA-
TION: RETAIL STORES, OFFICES, BANKS,
HOTELS, THEATRES

AREAS OF LESS COMMERCIAL CONCENTRATION:
GARAGES, FILLING STATIONS, AND RETAIL
SHOPS NOT ELSEWHERE INCLUDED

WHOLESALE COMMERCIAL ESTABLISHMENTS

RETAIL SHOPS AND RESIDENCES IN THE
SAME BUILDINGS

RESIDENCES, INCLUDING LODGING-HOUSES

BUILDINGS USED FOR COMMERCIAL STORAGE

PUBLIC BUILDINGS: LIBRARY, CHURCHES
SCHOOLS, GOVERNMENT BUILDINGS ETC.

MOTOR BUS TERMINALS

PARKS

OPEN SPACES USED FOR PARKING

OPEN SPACES WHERE FACTORIES HAVE
RECENTLY BEEN DESTROYED

SCALE   0'   250'   500'

FIG. 4. LOOKING UP THE CONCORD RIVER FROM THE BRIDGE AT ROGERS STREET TOWARD THE MILLS NEAR THE LAWRENCE STREET BRIDGE.

FIG. 5. MILLS OF THE MASSACHUSETTS MOHAIR PLUSH COMPANY, ONE OF THE SERIES OF MILLS BORDERING THE BOSTON AND MAINE RAILROAD.

11

FIG. 6. NEAR THE SUMMIT OF FORT HILL, ROGERS FORT HILL PARK; LOOKING SOUTHWARD UP THE CONCORD.

FIG. 7. THE DAM AT THE HEAD OF PAWTUCKET FALLS.

FIG. 8. CORPORATION-BUILT LODGINGHOUSES ON DUTTON STREET.

FIG. 9. THE LOWELL TEXTILE SCHOOL AS SEEN FROM THE SOUTH
BANK OF THE MERRIMACK.

13

Moody Street just north of the Merrimack [Map
II and Fig. 9]) is a symbol of the importance of
technical training to an industrial city. One familiar
with the early history of manufactures in New England is reminded by certain of the street names of
Lowell of the city's significance in industry, for
Jackson, Appleton, Worthen, Moody, Dutton, and
Lawrence, as well as Lowell itself, are names of men
who ranked among the industrial pioneers of the
early decades of the nineteenth century. Even the
architecture of Lowell conveys a hint as to the city's
fundamentally industrial character. With the exception of a cluster of houses in Middlesex Village
(Map II) there are few examples of the attractive
houses of Colonial or very early nineteenth-century
types which give charm to many New England
towns. What is not modern in Lowell belongs for
the most part to that period in American architecture which began in the second quarter of the nineteenth century. It is clear that the present character
of the residential districts is the product of the period
since 1825, a period which coincides with the industrial era in New England's history.

It is apparent to one passing through the streets
of Lowell that large sections of the city are occupied
by a population of foreign origin. On Dutton Street
near the Merrimack mills is a long row of lodginghouses where almost every placard bears a French
name (Map III and Fig. 8) ; on various other streets
French names on shops or French street names—

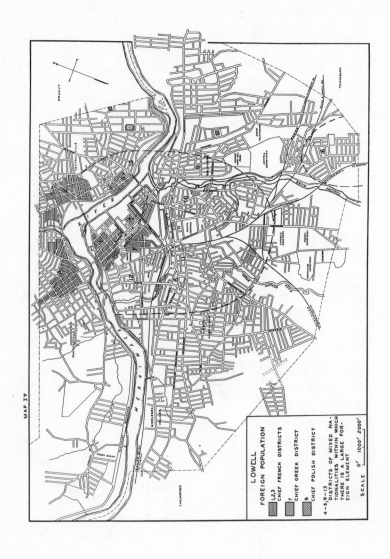

MAP IV

LOWELL
FOREIGN POPULATION

1,2,3
CHIEF FRENCH DISTRICTS

7
CHIEF GREEK DISTRICT

8
CHIEF POLISH DISTRICT

4-6,9-13
DISTRICTS OF MIXED NA-
TIONALITIES WITHIN WHICH
THERE IS A LARGE FOR-
EIGN ELEMENT

SCALE   0'   1000' 2000'

Boisvert, Beaulieu, Beaudry, for example—suggest the nationality of the surrounding community. Except for the areas occupied by mills, practically the whole quadrangle between Salem Street, Suffolk Street, and the Merrimack River houses a population of French Canadian origin (Map IV, District 1). The district is known as "Little Canada." This large French colony near the heart of the city is connected by the Aiken Street and Moody Street bridges with areas of French population no less extensive north of the Merrimack River (Map IV, Districts 2, 3). Each of these three districts has its French Roman Catholic church, its parochial school or schools, and its business quarter with numerous French shops. Besides these areas throughout which the French element in the population is strongly dominant, there are other areas in which there are many French among people of other nationalities. Some of these areas of mixed population adjoin the districts of compact French settlement. An example is the area north of Merrimack Street between Suffolk and Dutton (District 4). Other districts in which many French are scattered are in widely separated parts of the city. For example, there are considerable numbers of French near the church and school of Notre Dame de Lourdes, which is on Middlesex Street a short distance east of School Street (District 5), and others in the extreme southeastern section of the city (south of Lawrence Street and east of the Concord River [District 6]) near the church and school of Sainte Marie. That French influence has penetrated into the central business district of Lowell on Merrimack Street is shown by such names as the Mongeau Building, the Chalifoux Building, the Gagnon Company; it is doubtless in appeal to the important French element in the population that one of the few large department stores of the city is called the Bon Marché. The people of Canadian birth and the native-born of Canadian parentage together made up more than one-fourth of the population of Lowell in 1930.[1] These were in large part French Canadian.

A Greek colony occupies the greater part of the area between the North Common, Merrimack Street, and Dutton Street (District 7). Market Street is the chief business thoroughfare of this district. As many as a dozen Greek coffeehouses may be counted within a few blocks on Market Street, while Greek grocery, fruit, liquor, and dry goods stores, butcher, barber, and shoe repair shops handle much of the retail trade of an almost exclusively Greek community. Like the French, Greeks are also scattered in other areas among peoples of other nationalities. The area between District 7 and District 1 contains a mixture of French and Greek.

The Polish constitute a significant element in the population. Many of them live in a compact colony

---

[1] U. S. Bureau of the Census, *Fifteenth Census of the United States: 1930. Population,* Vol. II (Washington: Government Printing Office, 1933), pp. 250, 323.

in Centralville just west of Bridge Street along the river front (District 8). The Polish National Church is in this district. They are also numerous near a second Polish Catholic church located in the area immediately east of the Concord River between Rogers and East Merrimack Streets (District 9). This district they share with Lithuanians, Russians, and various other peoples. They are scattered also in other areas of mixed nationalities.

The district bordering the South Common and extending between it and the Concord (District 10) contains the chief Portuguese quarter, but in no part of it are the Portuguese unmixed with other people. They share the area with Italians, Poles, Armenians, Irish, and others. The Armenians have their church near the northern end of Lawrence Street and are scattered in territory west of this. A small cluster of Portuguese is found near the Merrimack mills, on Colburn and Tilden Streets (Map III). Jews tend to congregate in the district just west of the railroad near the northern end of Chelmsford Street (District 11), where there are three Jewish synagogues.

Some of the other foreign elements in the Lowell population are Swedish, Norwegian, German, Syrian, and Chinese. Among the English-speaking people are included large numbers of English and Irish. The Irish Free State ranks second only to Canada as a source of foreign-born population in Lowell, and people of Irish birth and the native-born of Irish parentage together constituted nearly one-sixth of the population in 1930.[1] Something of their importance is suggested by the fact that in addition to the French, Polish, and Lithuanian churches there are eight other Roman Catholic churches in Lowell. The Irish are widely scattered through the city.

Besides the foreign districts discussed, other districts of mixed nationalities in which the foreign element is large are the district between the Pawtucket Canal on the west and the Greek quarter and Little Canada on the east (District 12), and the area immediately north of the Merrimack and east of Bridge Street (District 13). The discussion has made it apparent that the central part and much of the northern part of the city are dominantly foreign. The census of 1930 shows that, of the 100,234 people then constituting the population of Lowell, 73 per cent were foreign born or of foreign parentage.[2] Of the larger cities of the United States—those having a population of more than 100,000—only four exceeded Lowell in the percentage of population foreign born or of foreign parentage. These were the industrial cities of Fall River and New Bedford, with 78 and 77 per cent, Paterson, New Jersey, another industrial city, which surpassed Lowell by only a fraction of 1 per cent, and, also exceeding Lowell by less than 1 per cent, the chief port of

[1] *Ibid.,* pp. 248, 323.   [2] *Ibid.,* p. 76.

FIG. 10. TENEMENTS ALONG THE NORTHERN CANAL, "LITTLE CANADA."

FIG. 11. TENEMENTS NEAR THE NORTH COMMON.

19

entry for immigrants, as well as a city of many industries, New York.[1] It is through the attraction of its mills that Lowell has come to have so large a foreign population.

Lowell exhibits evidences of the poverty, and also of the wealth, which may well belong to a mill city. Block after block of dingy wooden tenements (Figs. 10, 11) and long rows of shabby shops with dismal living quarters in the stories above them characterize many districts, while vast wooden buildings housing many families (Fig. 12) and some truly wretched dwellings (Fig. 13) occur in certain portions of the foreign quarters. Miles of streets are lined with drab and cheerless tenements, with dreary three- and four-story wooden apartment buildings, with poor crowded cottages, or with once good houses now decaying and shabby. Map II shows the extent of the poorest residential quarters. To these should be added most of the areas shown as mixed business and residence, for these consist in large part of shops with poor living quarters above them. There are few sharp dividing lines, and many areas classed as intermediate, adjoining the poorer areas, are scarcely distinguishable from them, while, on the other hand, other intermediate areas closely approach those classed as good. The areas of poor and low intermediate quality are large, and by some routes a traveler might cross the city from north to

[1] *Ibid.,* pp. 73–79.

FIG. 12. ONE OF THE LARGE WOODEN TENEMENT BUILDINGS IN
THE FRENCH DISTRICT NORTH OF THE AIKEN STREET BRIDGE.

FIG. 13. POOR TENEMENTS ON MARKET STREET.

FIG. 14. A HOUSE TYPICAL OF THE HILL DISTRICT
OF EASTERN BELVIDERE.

FIG. 15. A RESIDENCE ON ANDOVER STREET.

FIG. 16. IN THE HIGHLANDS RESIDENTIAL DISTRICT.

FIG. 17. MODERN HOMES IN THE WESTERN PORTION OF THE HIGHLANDS.

23

south seeing little which relieved the disheartening impression of dreariness.

But Lowell has in its outer sections many beautiful homes (Figs. 14, 15), wide tree-bordered avenues lined with spacious houses and pleasant lawns (Fig. 16), trim new residential quarters with attractive modern houses (Fig. 17), areas occupied by modest but neat and comfortable cottages. The larger residential districts of high quality are in the Highlands and eastern Belvidere (Map II), with smaller areas in Centralville and along the river front in Pawtucketville. Comfortable areas of intermediate quality in part adjoin these districts, while others in the southern part of the city are detached from them. Substantial schools and churches are widely distributed, and dignified public buildings grace the central section of the city (Figs. 9, 18, 19). Considerable areas are devoted to parks and playgrounds (Map II). Some of these are little improved, merely bare spaces for play, but Rogers Fort Hill Park is an attractive pleasure ground (Fig. 6), while North and South Commons (Fig. 20) afford pleasant areas of grass and trees in the most congested districts of the city.

Contrasts such as those revealed by Figures 10–17 are, of course, common to most cities. It is not the existence of these contrasts but, rather, the exceptionally large areas which are occupied by the mean and unattractive parts which help to mark Lowell as, in large degree, a mill workers' city.

FIG. 18. ST. ANNE'S CHURCH.

FIG. 19. MEMORIAL AUDITORIUM, EAST MERRIMACK STREET AT
CONCORD RIVER BRIDGE.

25

FIG. 20. THE SOUTH COMMON.

FIG. 21. THE HEART OF THE BUSINESS DISTRICT, MERRIMACK
STREET.

Lowell's industrial origin is reflected even in the city's pattern. The adjustments which the city has made to the topographic features of its site are the adjustments of a city in which industry was of primary importance. The locations of the major mill groups were indicated by topography, and the remainder of the city developed in conformity with the pattern thus initiated. The topographic features involved will be reserved for later discussion, but it seems apparent from a study of Map II that the semicircle of mills bordering the Merrimack and the Pawtucket Canal constitutes a nuclear ring within and around which the city grew. Within the semicircle are the chief retail business district (Fig. 21), centering at the intersection of Merrimack and Central Streets, one of the wholesale districts, on Market and Middle Streets, and, farther west on Merrimack Street, the major civic center (Map III). Encircling the nucleus are the residential regions. From it the main thoroughfares radiate in all directions, and lesser retail trade districts are aligned along these thoroughfares. In general, the poorer residence districts are massed near the mills, and the good residence districts are those far removed from the industrial areas, though there are topographic factors which affect this relationship. The convenience of having workers housed near the factories accounts for considerable blocks of residential property in the innermost section of the city. The concentration of mills in the heart of Lowell and the radial pattern of the city focusing upon this central mill district clearly suggest that we have here an illustration not of a city which has attracted mills, but of mills around which has developed a city.

Evidences of Change

The difficulties which have beset Lowell's industries during recent years have left their scars upon the city. The most conspicuous evidences are the several spaces once occupied by factories now lying open and unused. Foundation walls or occasional heaps of discarded brick or stone show where some of the former buildings stood. Several such open spaces in the heart of the city are shown on Map III, and additional areas are indicated on Map II. The largest two areas are the space just east of Dutton Street and south of Market Street, and that to the east of Gorham Street and immediately south of River Meadow Brook. Map III shows, just south of Market Street, the site of a former mill building now utilized for parking.

In other cases former mills no longer occupied by manufacturing stand vacant or are used for other purposes. Note on Map V the vacant mills at the junction of Broadway and Pawtucket Street, the several vacant units in the mill group at the junction of the Concord River and River Meadow Brook, and the smaller vacant factories elsewhere in the city. Note on Map III the large buildings on Bridge Street and south of Market Street used for commer-

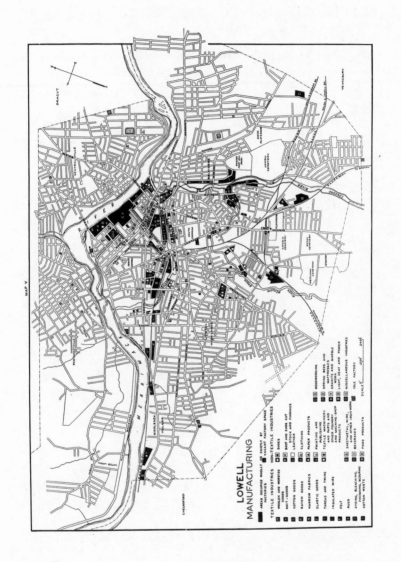

MAP V

LOWELL
MANUFACTURING

■ AREAS OCCUPIED WHOLLY
OR CHIEFLY BY
FACTORIES

☐ VACANT FACTORY SPACE

TEXTILE INDUSTRIES   NON-TEXTILE INDUSTRIES

WOOLEN AND WORSTED
GOODS   SHOES

KNIT-GOODS   BOOT AND SHOE CUT
                          STOCK AND FINDINGS
COTTON GOODS
                          LEATHER
RAYON GOODS
                          CLOTHING
NARROW FABRICS
                          PAPER PRODUCTS
ELASTIC GOODS
                          PRINTING AND
THREAD AND TWINE   PUBLISHING

INSULATED WIRE   TEXTILE MACHINERY
                          AND PARTS AND
FELT   OTHER FOUNDRY
                          AND MACHINE-SHOP
RUGS   PRODUCTS

DYEING, BLEACHING,   SHEET-METAL, WIRE
FINISHING, SCOURING   AND OTHER IRON WORK

COTTON WASTE   MISCELLANEOUS INDUSTRIES

                          BEVERAGES

                          FOOD PRODUCTS

                          WOODWORKING

                          SPRING BEDS AND
                          MATTRESSES

                          GRANITE AND MARBLE
                          WORK

                          LIGHT, HEAT AND POWER

                          IDLE FACTORY

SCALE

cial storage, and also the buildings in the Bridge
Street and Market Street mill groups devoted to
other commercial purposes. These buildings were
formerly parts of the adjacent manufacturing establishments. Those on Market Street have been converted into garages, while a dealer in automobile
accessories occupies the Bridge Street building. A
motor sales company is established in a former ten-
story mill building on Jackson Street now reduced
to two stories, and a large mill on Dutton Street
just south of Broadway is occupied by The Giant
Store, a number of small concerns each with a booth
of its own, offering a great variety of commodities
for retail sale.

In still other cases large mill groups which formerly housed a single manufacturing company are
now occupied by many smaller concerns, either
wholly by manufacturing companies or by a mixture
of manufacturing and commercial concerns. This
is true of several of the mill groups making up the
"inner ring" of factories. Note on Map V the varied
industries clustering in the mills on Jackson Street,
Market Street, Bridge Street, and at the junction
of the Pawtucket Canal with the Concord River,
and also the several manufacturing companies in the
large mill unit on Chelmsford Street. This map gives
an incomplete impression of the number of companies involved, since one symbol may represent several manufacturers of the same class. For example,
the group of mills in the space between Bridge

Street, Canal Street, the Merrimack and Concord
Rivers, and the post office (Map III), formerly
constituting the Massachusetts Cotton Mills, in
spite of the demolition of some units of the group,
now houses more than thirty industrial and commercial companies. There are, in addition, 300,000
square feet of unoccupied floor space available for
rent. Note on Map V that in most of the mill groups
bordering the Merrimack and the eastern part of
the Pawtucket Canal there is some vacant floor space
in addition to the occupied areas.

The commercial and residential areas also give
testimony as to recent changes. Vacant shops and
vacant tenements are many. It is, however, chiefly
small shops in the poorer districts which have been
vacated, and in the commercial districts of better
quality on Merrimack and Central Streets there is
little indication of change. Shop windows are bright
with attractive displays, traffic is congested, throngs
crowd the streets on Saturday mill holidays, and
lack of prosperity, however felt, is not in evidence.

In Little Canada evidences of loss of population,
or of its removal from the central portion of the city,
are conspicuous. Once a highly congested district,
it is now sprinkled with open plots. These are in
large part owned by banks.[1] The buildings removed
from them were, in general, poor, and their destruction doubtless was in most cases desirable, but that

---

[1] *Property Atlas of the City of Lowell* (Philadelphia: Franklin
Survey Co., 1936).

the areas remain open so near the heart of the city is telling evidence of the lessened demand for space in this quarter.

Certain residential districts show signs of decay, which must, however, be attributed in part to the earlier industrial expansion of the city rather than to lowered prosperity in recent years. Much of the Highlands residential area (Map II) is occupied by great old houses surrounded by wide lawns and fine trees. But in the eastern part of the area not a few of the fine old houses are now shabby. Some have been converted into apartment houses. Doubtless many have been abandoned by their former owners as the conditions which belong to the industrial heart of the city crept too close upon them from the north and east. Similar decay naturally occurred earlier in areas nearer the center of the city. Highland Street, which forms the southern margin of the South Common, is lined by roomy old houses, some of them now shabby. It commands a pleasant view across the common and was once part of a good residential quarter. It has become an island in a sea of tenements. Similar pressure of expanding tenement districts upon good residential areas is apparent in the residential quarters of the northeast. It is clear that much of the area north of the Merrimack and east of Bridge Street was once a good residential district. The southern part of it near the bridge has been taken over by a poorer class of residents, and deterioration tends to spread northward. Along

Mammoth Road, the continuation of School Street north of the river, are other illustrations of large old houses now showing signs of deterioration. Pawtucket Street near School Street shows similar evidences of loss. Attractive new residential quarters have developed in the western part of the Highlands and along eastern Andover Street in Belvidere, yet the impression left by a survey of the residential districts is that the wealth of Lowell was rather more of yesterday than of today, for the partial decay of some of the older, richer, residential areas seems scarcely to have been compensated for by the development of new ones of like quality.

The Present Industrial Pattern

Despite many losses Lowell's industries present today a complex and varied picture. Though the city is one of diverse industries, it is primarily a textile city still, four textile manufactures, woolen and worsted goods, knit goods, cotton goods, and rayon goods, constituting in 1936 by value the four leading manufactured products. The manufacture of shoes closely follows rayon manufacture in value of products, and the tanning and finishing of leather ranks sixth among the city's industries. Data for the rayon and leather industries cannot be presented separately by the State Department of Labor and Industries without disclosing the operations of individual establishments. Data for the other major industries are presented in Table 1.

TABLE 1

Manufactures of Lowell in 1936*

Principal Industries	Value of Materials Used	Amount of Wages Paid	Average Number of Wage Earners Employed	Value of Products
All industries......	$33,542,740	$14,101,690	15,832	$63,818,047
Woolen and worsted goods...........	7,661,482	2,313,230	2,560	11,783,309
Knit goods........	3,824,034	1,906,935	2,710	7,433,200
Cotton goods......	3,169,579	2,284,380	2,878	7,041,821
Rayon goods......	....	....	.....	....
Boots and shoes....	2,465,820	1,585,956	1,892	5,356,340
Leather, tanned, curried and finished...........	....	....	.....	....
Printing and publishing.........	1,025,464	779,739	551	3,200,998
Bread and other bakery products.	1,659,264	365,836	390	2,583,442
Textile machinery and parts.......	622,455	275,469	244	1,221,034
Boot and shoe cut stock and findings	538,760	199,283	247	902,337
Clothing, women's.	323,383	110,254	149	560,208
Cotton small wares.	298,539	146,731	166	530,737
Foundry and machine shop products........	102,144	115,210	92	287,033
Boxes, paper.......	86,821	61,081	63	193,453
Confectionery......	104,262	33,276	33	186,081
Beverages.........	31,753	13,094	13	93,674
Other industries...	11,628,980	3,911,216	3,844	22,444,380

* Commonwealth of Massachusetts, "Census of Manufactures, 1936, City of Lowell," p. 1.

Worsted manufacture in Lowell, excluding the manufacture of worsted yarn by one knitting company, is carried on by six companies; there is, in addition, a small weave shop making handwoven blankets. One of the six companies is primarily a manufacturer of mohair plush, a material widely used for upholstery, especially for seats in trains, but manufactures also worsted yarns. It dyes and finishes its own products. A second company produces worsted men's wear and dress goods, carrying on in its several mills all the processes from the raw wool to the finished cloth. Bunting is a minor product of this establishment. Controlled by the same interests as this company and managed in co-operation with it is a third concern producing yarns only. Of the remaining companies, which operate entirely independently, two are yarn manufacturers, doing no weaving, while the third has only a weaving department in Lowell, operating other mills elsewhere. It manufactures worsted dress goods and suitings. One of the yarn companies makes not only worsted but high-grade mohair yarns much used in the manufacture of automobile upholstery.

The six companies have a total of approximately 70,000 spinning spindles, 15,000 twisting spindles, and 650 looms.[1] There is among the worsted factories no very large single unit. Numbers normally

---

[1] Totals calculated from figures in *Official American Textile Directory, 1937* and *Official Statistics of Textile Corporations, American Wool and Cotton Reporter,* January 20, 1938, Section 2.

employed range from about 75 in the smallest establishment to some 850 in the largest. Three of the companies operate factories in other cities or towns in addition to their establishments in Lowell.

The knit-goods industry in Lowell is varied. The largest company is a former manufacturer of cotton cloth which shifted to the manufacture of knit goods late in the nineteenth century. It continues to spin cotton yarn, operating 57,000 cotton spindles and selling cotton hosiery yarns. It buys worsted, mercerized, and rayon yarns and knits cotton underwear, knit tubing and underwear cloth, jersey cloth, sweaters, and a variety of knitted fabrics in cotton, rayon, wool, and worsted. In addition to knitting machines, it operates about 1,000 sewing machines. It dyes, bleaches, and finishes its own products.

A second large establishment is devoted to the manufacture of knitted outerwear chiefly of woolen and worsted. It spins woolen and worsted yarns for its own use, operating 5,000 worsted and 3,000 woolen spindles. No dyeing is done, the wool being for the most part top dyed before spinning. The chief products are sweaters, bathing suits, sports coats, and jersey cloth. These two companies together employ normally about 2,000 workers, at maximum capacity about 2,500.

Two smaller establishments, employing from 70 to 100 workers each, manufacture sweaters and bathing suits. They buy all the yarns used. Three other companies manufacture hosiery, one making hosiery

for children, one, boys' sport hose, and one, men's
seamless half hose. Cotton, rayon, worsted, and acetate yarns all are utilized. Yarns are bought. The
largest of the three operates a dyeing and bleaching
department. The three together employ normally
about 680 workers. Besides these companies which
are primarily knit-goods manufacturers, some knitting is done by one establishment classified as a clothing manufacturer.

There are now operating in Lowell only two companies weaving cotton cloth, the Merrimack Manufacturing Company and the Boott Mills (Map III).
The company spinning cotton yarns for the knit-
goods industry has been previously described. In
addition, the Nashua Manufacturing Company,
whose main plant is in Nashua, New Hampshire,
owns in Lowell the Suffolk Mills, which are equipped
for the manufacture of cotton blankets. The Suffolk
Mills have been idle since 1936 but have not been
dismantled. The two operating cotton-goods manufacturers are large concerns having, together, about
180,000 cotton spindles and 6,000 looms.[1] The idle
Suffolk Mills are equipped with about 38,000
spindles and 500 looms.[2] Of the operating mills, one
specializes in the manufacture of corduroys and velveteens. It dyes, bleaches, and finishes its products.
The other is a variety mill producing a wide range
of fabrics; towels, toweling, curtains and curtain

[1] *Official American Textile Directory, 1937*, pp. 140–141.
[2] *Ibid.*, p. 142.

scrims, nets, voiles, and marquisettes in white and colors are important products; the company also manufactures corduroys, velveteens, twills, gabardines, sateen, poplin, sheeting, shirting, pique, duck, and various other fabrics. This mill does a part of its own bleaching and finishing. It sells yarn and twine as well as cloth and does needlework to requirements on the fabrics manufactured.

The Waterhead Mills, Incorporated, well known as a producer of corduroys, is a corduroy-converting company. It weaves no cloth but buys the gray goods, finishes them, and sells them under its own trade brands.

The products of Lowell's rayon industry include staple goods such as taffetas, satins, and twills, and also fabrics of fancy weaves. Both acetate and viscose rayons are used. The industry is represented by two companies, the Newmarket Manufacturing Company (Map III) and the Wannalancit Textile Company, a smaller establishment. The two together employ about 1,000 operatives and have more than 2,000 looms. Neither company dyes its products.

Besides the four major textile manufactures, there are various lesser textile industries, data for most of which are not shown separately in Table 1. There are several manufacturers of narrow fabrics such as tapes, bindings, and ribbons ("Cotton small wares," Table 1). Of these, one company manufactures woven cotton tapes and webbings for industrial purposes. Some are used on spinning and twister frames in textile mills, others for printing press tape-bands and for binding books and carpets. A second company weaves cotton, silk, and rayon tapes used for shoe bindings; a third makes braided silk and cotton shoe and corset laces; and a fourth, tinsel ribbons and cords. All yarns used are purchased. A fifth company makes bias binding from woven cotton fabrics. These are companies employing between 20 and 50 workers each.

Two establishments manufacture insulated wire —lamp cords, telephone cords, and cables. About 1,300 braiding machines [1] are operated, and about 125 to 150 workers are employed. Yarns are purchased, cotton, rayon, linen, woolen, and silk all being utilized. Two companies make elastic goods, one making covered rubber thread, the other, various types of elastic webbing in cotton and rayon. About 115 workers are employed. One substantial concern manufactures cotton sewing thread. It buys yarn, utilizes 6,000 twister spindles,[2] bleaches, dyes, and finishes. A smaller company manufactures twine.

Completing the textile picture are one wool-scouring company, one dye works, two felting companies, one rug manufacturer, and three companies processing cotton waste. The wool-scouring company is one of some ten establishments in the country which carbonize as well as scour wool on commission. It

---

[1] *Ibid.*, p. 141.   [2] *Ibid.*

operates also a garnetting department. This company has shown rapid growth and employs in a favorable season as many as 170 workers. The dye works is a relatively small establishment. It dyes yarns, narrow fabrics, and hosiery on commission. The felting companies manufacture sheet felts and felt polishing wheels. They employ together about 35 workers. The rug company is a small establishment making rag rugs. The business of handling cotton waste has, of course, been adversely affected by the decline of Lowell's cotton industry. About 130 workers are normally employed, but operations are now on a reduced basis.

It should be noted that the towns bordering Lowell have also textile establishments which are near enough to function as parts of the Lowell textile community. For example, a short distance beyond the Lowell border in Dracut (Map II), and until recently located within Lowell, is a substantial establishment for the dyeing and printing of wool tops. Chelmsford, which adjoins Lowell on the west and south, has important wool-scouring and wool-combing industries.

Between the textile industries and clothing manufacture, distinctions are difficult to draw, since the knit-goods industries produce finished clothing. Establishments classed as clothing manufacturers are those which primarily cut clothing from fabrics rather than manufacturing fabrics, but such establishments may knit clothing in addition, while com-

panies making chiefly knitted bathing suits, for example, may make suits of woven fabrics as well.
Three manufacturers are represented by the data
presented in Table 1 for women's clothing. In addition, there is one company manufacturing leather
and woolen sportswear for men and boys and one
manufacturer of children's clothing, chiefly play
suits and snow suits, some of which are made of piece
goods, while others are knitted. These two companies, when operating normally, employ, together,
265 workers. There are two companies making hats
and caps on a small scale, one for local sale only, the
other for a wider market. Ten workers are employed.

Shoe manufacture is an industry in which shifts
of location are frequent. Companies come and go
and the picture changes with surprising rapidity.
What is said of the industry at any one location today is likely to be untrue tomorrow. The statistics
presented for the manufacture of boots and shoes in
Table 1 represent the ten shoe companies operating
in Lowell in 1936. There are also ten companies in
the city today, only seven of which, however, were
there in 1936. Statistics were not obtainable from
all of these companies, but it is estimated on the basis
of those available that the production capacity of
these ten companies is not far from 30,000 [1] pairs of
shoes daily. The largest establishment normally pro-

---

[1] Data obtained in part from *Blue Book of the Shoe and Leather
Industries* (1936–37 edition; Chicago: Hide and Leather Publishing
Co., 1936), pp. 93–94.

duces from 4,000 to 5,000 pairs daily, one of the smaller ones 900 to 1,000 pairs. Numbers employed per company range from fewer than 100 to about 500. Women's and children's shoes of cheap and medium grades are the chief products. One company manufactures house slippers.

The American Hide and Leather Company, the world's greatest producer of fine upper leathers, operates in Lowell one of the larger tanneries of the world.[1] Seventeen different leathers, used for shoe uppers, handbags, and inner soles, are tanned and finished. These include various styles and colors in calf, suede, buck, and patent leathers.[2] Several hundred workers are employed.[3] The tanning industry in Lowell is entirely in the hands of this company.

Also associated with the shoe industry is the production of various supplies used by shoe manufacturers (Boot and shoe cut stock and findings, Table 1). These products are varied. Two textile companies manufacturing shoe bindings and shoelaces have previously been noted. The manufactures of the six other companies include wood heels, cut lifts, counters, box toes, leather insoles, and leather board.

Printing and publishing, which ranks next after the leather industry in value of products (Table 1), is, of course, an industry of importance in every considerable city. The industry in Lowell, however, has

---

[1] *Lowell Courier Citizen,* Lowell Centennial Edition, June 30, 1936, p. 4a.

[2] *Ibid.,* p. 39a.   [3] *Ibid.,* p. 3a.

a slightly greater importance as compared with other industries than it has in Massachusetts as a whole. The value of the products of printing and publishing in Lowell constituted in 1936 about 5 per cent of the city's total value of manufactured products; in the state as a whole, printing and publishing accounted for 3.6 per cent of the total value of products.[1]

Several newspapers serve Lowell's foreign population, *L'Etoile,* a daily paper, *Le Citoyen* and *Le Clairon,* published by another company, and the *New England Greek Messenger.* The English dailies are the *Lowell Courier Citizen* and the *Lowell Evening Leader,* published by the Courier Citizen Company, and the *Lowell Sun.* The *Lowell Sunday Telegram* is a weekly publication.

In addition to commercial printing by the six newspaper companies, commercial printing is done in twenty-seven other establishments. Some of these are very small concerns. Only fourteen printers and publishers operated plants large enough to be included in the published statistics for the industry (Table 1). Printing of paper boxes, of bags and wrapping paper, of stationery, and of advertising are branches of the industry upon which certain companies concentrate. One concern which com-

---

[1] Commonwealth of Massachusetts, Department of Labor and Industries, Division of Statistics, "Census of Manufactures in Massachusetts, 1936, Summary by Industries" (Mfrs., 1936: No. 44, mimeographed), pp. 1, 6.

mands a large per cent of its market outside Lowell
specializes in race-track printing. The largest printing plant is that of the Courier Citizen Company. In
addition to the building used for publishing, the company occupies two of the mills of a former cotton
corporation. It maintains a large lithographic department; it prints all the telephone directories used
in New England.[1] In addition to the printing establishments, the city has a modern electrotype foundry.

The manufacture of bread and other bakery products (Table 1) is, of course, also an industry which
in large part supplies local demand and which is common to every city. In Lowell, bakery products constituted in 1936 4 per cent of the total value of all
manufactured products; in the state, bakery products constituted 3.1 per cent of the value of all manufactured products.[2] Thirty-five bakeries were represented in the data presented in Table 1. Most of
these are small shops baking only for their own retail
trade. There are several relatively small wholesale
bakeries. Two establishments are outstanding and
command a wide market for their products. One is
the Megowen Educator Food Company, which operates in one of the former cotton mills what is reputed
to be the largest baking plant in New England,
manufacturing Toasterettes, Crax, and other crack-
ers and cookies. The other is a company which main-

---

[1] *Lowell Courier Citizen, op. cit.,* p. 36a.
[2] Commonwealth of Massachusetts, "Census of Manufactures, 1936,
Summary by Industries," pp. 1, 2.

tains in various cities and towns more than fifty retail shops and also distributes widely through other retail stores; this retail trade is supplied by four bakeries, one of which is in Lowell.[1] The products are bread, cakes, pies, pastries, and baked beans.[2] In addition, several baking companies whose bakeries are located elsewhere maintain in Lowell facilities for storage and distribution.

Although the manufacture of textile machinery and parts has declined greatly in Lowell, it still produces a wide variety of products. The establishments now operating are concerns of modest size, most of them employing not more than 50 workers and some fewer than 10. One company manufactures machinery and tanks for use in dyeing raw stock and in dyeing and finishing woven and knitted fabrics. Another makes drying machines and other equipment for textile finishing plants.[3] One builds warping machines, that is, machines for putting warp on looms. This company has developed in recent years a high-speed warper for use in cotton mills and, in somewhat modified form, in rayon mills. One company builds all kinds of special machinery on order; woodworking as well as textile machinery is made. Another specializes in ventilation and dust-collection equipment for textile mills, cotton- and wool-blow-

---

[1] *Lowell Courier Citizen, op. cit.,* p. 40a.

[2] *Ibid.*

[3] O. L. Stone, *History of Massachusetts Industries* (Chicago: S. J. Clarke Publishing Co., 1930), I, 761.

ing systems, dyehouse and vapor-exhausting systems.[1] Still another makes shoddy pickers, machines used to tear rags apart, reducing them to fibrous state so that they may be reworked into cloth again. The manufacturers of textile parts include one establishment making loom reeds and slasher combs, one manufacturer of card clothing, and one maker of textile pins. This last establishment makes also phonograph needles. There are two manufacturers of bobbins, spools, and shuttles.

Several other companies repair textile machinery. Roll covering, that is, the re-covering with leather of rolls in textile mills, is done by three companies. Two of these also make and repair machine brushes. One manufactures, in addition, a machine by which roll covering is done and makes leather belting and leather aprons for textile work.[2] Others do general machine repair work. Not machinists, but closely associated with the machine industries, are two additional small companies making leather belting, and one manufacturing leather cement.

In addition to the manufacturers of textile machinery are one company manufacturing woodworking machinery and another making machinery for tire repairing, one pump manufacturer, and one manufacturer of scales (Foundry and machine-shop products, Table 1). One company makes machine knives used by paper mills, leather manufacturers,

---

[1] *Ibid.*, p. 763.
[2] *Lowell Courier Citizen, op. cit.*, pp. 3a, 29a.

woodworking plants, feed mills, and by a great variety of other industries. This is the oldest machine knife factory in the United States. Foundries consist of two iron foundries and one small brass and aluminum foundry. One establishment employing from 20 to 60 workers manufactures steam boilers.

Data for other metal workers are not shown separately in Table 1. They include two wire manufacturers, a screw manufacturer, and a dozen companies or individuals doing sheet-metal work or other ironwork. Most of these maintain only very small plants.

The manufacture of paper products occupies nine companies. Only three are represented in the data given for paper boxes in Table 1. Other products of these companies include paper cores and cones for winding cloth, yarn, ribbon, and paper; paper mailing cases; and paper tubes of many sizes used for a great variety of purposes. Many varieties of round boxes, as well as shoe cartons, folding boxes, corrugated boxes, and boxes of other types, are manufactured. The largest plant reports approximately 100 normally employed.

There are four manufacturing confectioners (Table 1). Of the larger two, one manufactures only for its own retail establishment in Lowell in which it operates also a restaurant and soda fountain. The other markets 70 per cent of its product in other cities. The smaller concerns serve almost exclusively a Lowell market.

Beverage manufacturers consist of one brewery, a

Coca-Cola bottling company, and four bottlers of carbonated beverages. The data shown in Table 1 for this industry are not representative, as the brewery is a large establishment employing, when in normal operation, more than 200 workers, and the numbers reported as now employed by other companies exceed the total given in Table 1.

Under the heading "Other industries" in Table 1 are included statistics for the lesser industries and also for more important industries for which data cannot be presented separately. The cases of rayon and leather have already been discussed. Another important industry, represented by only one company, is the manufacture of electrical apparatus. The Heinze Electric Company manufactures automobile horns, automobile defrosters, fractional horsepower motors for heaters, and other electrical equipment. Another considerable, though smaller, establishment is that of the Imperial Upholstery Company, which manufactures furniture. Normal employment in these two factories amounts to 775 workers. A second furniture company, operating a smaller plant, manufactures bridge tables.

Lesser industries each of which is represented by three or more companies are other woodworking industries, the manufacture of spring beds and mattresses, granite and marble work, the manufacture of electric signs, and the making of ice cream. Woodworking is done by several lumber companies which operate mills in connection with their lumberyards and by one additional company engaged in cabinet-making. The granite and marble workers are manu-facturers of monuments and tombstones.

Various products the manufacture of which is in-cluded in Table 1 under the heading "Other indus-tries" have been discussed in connection with the major industries to which they are related. Other miscellaneous products, each manufactured by only one or two companies, include artificial limbs, awn-ings, automobile tops and bodies, calendars, chemi-cals, cigars, concrete garden furniture, corsets, cur-tains, ice, ink, ladders, medicines, mops, patterns, pencils, polish, perfumes, rubber stamps, rubber mats, safety treads for steps, toilet preparations, undertakers' supplies, vinegar, and window shades. Some of these products are manufactured by very small concerns, the plant being operated by the owner with few or no helpers. Others are the prod-ucts of larger establishments. The two companies manufacturing patent medicines are old and sub-stantial concerns. The companies manufacturing safety treads, corsets, and rubber mats are compa-nies employing between 15 and 60 workers each. Immediately south of the southern margin of Lowell is the Lowell Fertilizer Company employing at peak season nearly 100 workers.

Electric light, heat, and power are supplied by the Lowell Electric Light Corporation and gas by the Lowell Gas Light Company. Besides these public utilities companies there are companies which develop hydroelectric power from the Merrimack and Concord Rivers either for their own use in manufacturing or for sale to other manufacturers. The Wamesit Power Company and the Middlesex Company generate power at the falls of the Concord, own mill buildings near the power sites, and distribute power to their tenants. The power of the Merrimack River in Lowell is owned by a company known as "The Proprietors of Locks and Canals." This company is in turn controlled by other companies which own its stock and develop the power or lease their rights to associates for development. The companies generating power from the Merrimack do so separately in their individual plants, the Proprietors of Locks and Canals controlling the dam and canals and regulating the amounts of water drawn. Of these companies, some use the power which they develop for their own manufacturing. Others do not themselves manufacture but supply the electric power which they generate to manufacturers occupying the buildings which these companies own. Symbols for light, heat, and power companies on Map V indicate not only the plants of the public utilities companies and the headquarters of the Proprietors of Locks and Canals but also the locations of the power plants of those companies which supply power to their tenants. The complex power situation in Lowell results from the early history of industrial development and the recent industrial changes and will be subsequently explained.

The state census in 1936 counted 204 industrial establishments in Lowell of sufficient size to be included in the data presented.[1] The total value of Lowell's manufactured products constituted 2.2 per cent of the total value of products of all the industries of Massachusetts.[2] A comparison of the values of Lowell's leading products with the values of those products for the state shows that Lowell produced in 1936 5.6 per cent of the woolen and worsted goods, 6.5 per cent of the cotton goods, 21.5 per cent of the knit goods, and 3.7 per cent of the shoes produced in Massachusetts.[3] The position as to rayon goods can be estimated only approximately in the absence of an exact value for Lowell; on the basis of the rank of rayon goods in Lowell between cotton goods and boots and shoes, it is estimated that Lowell's product constituted not far from 15 per cent of the total value of silk and rayon goods for the state.[4]

Examining now the distribution of Lowell's industrial establishments (Map V), it is apparent that the textile industries are in large measure concentrated in the semicircle of mills bordering the Merrimack and the eastern portion of the Pawtucket Canal. Within this group are established both of the cotton companies, both of the rayon companies,

---

[1] Commonwealth of Massachusetts, "Census of Manufactures, 1936, City of Lowell," p. 1.

[2] Data for Massachusetts from Commonwealth of Massachusetts, "Census of Manufactures, 1936, Summary by Industries," p. 1.

[3] *Ibid.*, pp. 1, 3, 4, 7.

[4] *Ibid.*, p. 6.

all but one of the knitting companies, four of the six
major woolen and worsted mills, the felt and elastic
manufacturers, the wool-scouring plant, one dye
works, one company handling cotton waste, and one
twine manufacturer. A second group of textile
manufacturers, consisting of two woolen and worsted companies, one knitting company, and the corduroy-converting company, clusters near the junction of the Concord River and River Meadow Brook.
The one worsted mill south of this cluster, between
the Concord River and Gorham, Street, is a mill
belonging to one of the companies in the Concord
group; processes preliminary to spinning, such as
scouring and combing, are carried on there. The
manufacturers of narrow fabrics, all relatively small
establishments, and the plants making insulated wire
are widely scattered. One of each is in the area of
mixed manufacturing and commerce between
Broadway and the western portion of the Pawtucket
Canal, adjoining the major textile group. Others are
completely detached from both of the major textile
areas. Two of the waste companies also occupy detached positions. The plant of the thread-manufac-
turing company is on the Merrimack but in the
western part of the city well above the dam.

Of the clothing manufacturers, two are associated
with the major textile group, one with the Concord
group, one forms part of the small mill cluster on
Chelmsford Street, one is in the area of mixed manufacturing and commerce between Broadway and the

Pawtucket Canal, and the remaining ones are in areas which are primarily commercial.

Almost all of the manufacturers of shoes and of shoemakers' supplies are in that part of the central mill district which extends from the mouth of the Concord River to near the bridge crossing the Pawtucket Canal at Broadway. One shoe factory in the Chelmsford Street group and a heel factory on Pawtucket Street are exceptions. The plant of the American Hide and Leather Company forms part of the Concord mill area though on the opposite side of the river from the textile mills.

Small print shops are widely scattered in areas of trade and residence. The offices and publishing plants of the English newspapers are within the major area of retail trade, while the French publishing companies are on residential streets in areas with French population. Half a dozen printing and paper-ruling companies are concentrated on Middle Street (Map III) immediately adjoining the major district of retail trade. (Two or more companies of one kind at the same address are in most cases shown by only one symbol on Map V.) Several printing companies are housed in former cotton mills included in the central ring of factories.

The paper-products industry shows little concentration. Establishments are distributed between the central mill ring, the Concord industrial area, and the Chelmsford Street cluster.

The foundry and machine-shop industries, including textile machinery and parts, are chiefly in two districts, one the area south of Broadway adjoining the western portion of the Pawtucket Canal, the other an area in the southern part of the city near the railroad and River Meadow Brook. Several are in the more eastern and northern parts of the central mill ring. A few are scattered elsewhere. Sheet-metal workers are not concentrated in the major industrial districts. Their establishments are for the most part small and are scattered among shops in the lower-class commercial areas.

Bakeries for the most part avoid the industrial districts. They are scattered along streets of mixed shops and residences or in districts primarily residential. The exception is the large bakery previously described occupying a portion of the plant of a former cotton company within the central mill area. Only wholesale bakeries are shown on Map V. Several manufacturers of confectionery or ice cream belong to the central industrial ring. Others are in areas primarily commercial.

The bottlers, like the bakers, avoid the more concentrated industrial districts. The brewery is near the southern margin of the industrial and commercial area between the New York, New Haven, and Hartford Railroad and River Meadow Brook. One plant is on the fringe of the Concord industrial area. One forms a link in the chain of factories following the railroad in the western part of the city. Others are in commercial or residential areas.

Furniture and other woodworking industries belong in part to the central industrial area and in part are scattered elsewhere. The plant of the Imperial Upholstery Company is at the western margin of the city, constituting one of the chain of factories following the railroad. Another furniture company adjoins the railroad which follows the eastern bank of the Concord. The lumberyard and mill of one of the lumber companies flanks the Boston division of the Boston and Maine Railroad in the southern portion of the city. The manufacture of beds and bedding is divided between the central area and the River Meadow Brook area. Granite and marble works are located near the cemeteries and the railroads on Lawrence Street, Gorham Street, and to the west of Gorham Street.

Of the light and power companies, the electric light company's plant forms part of the industrial group bordering the lower Concord, the gas works are in the western section of the Pawtucket Canal area, while the companies generating power from the Merrimack and Concord Rivers must obviously be in the central and Concord industrial areas respectively. The symbol in the area inclosed by Dutton Street, Broadway, and the Suffolk Street canal marks the headquarters of the Proprietors of Locks and Canals.

Of the manufacturing establishments classed as "miscellaneous" on Map V, about half form part of the central industrial ring—though lack of space prevents showing separate symbols for each company. Most of the others, chiefly very small establishments, are scattered in nonindustrial areas. The Heinze Electric Company and the American Mason Safety Tread Company belong to the Concord manufacturing district.

In summary, it is clear that there are two concentrated industrial districts, the central semicircle and the area bordering the Concord, and, in addition, a series of industrial plants sprinkled along and near the railroads, and many small establishments scattered in areas primarily commercial or residential. The main railroad line through the city crosses and recrosses the Pawtucket Canal, thus traversing for a short distance the central mill district. Thus this district and the railroad industrial belt overlap, and the area bordering the western part of the Pawtucket Canal belongs to both. There is, in addition, a minor industrial cluster on Chelmsford Street. Within all of the industrial areas, production is varied, and, while the textile industries are for the most part concentrated in the two major districts, they share these districts, especially the central area, with many other industries. Factors contributing to an explanation of this industrial pattern will later be discussed.

The Commercial Districts

The picture which Lowell's commercial districts present is in no way striking. They are similar to those of other cities of its size. The major district of retail trade, which is the area containing the stores and shops in general of higher quality and larger size, and which also is the area of greatest commercial concentration, displays the usual array of department stores and smaller stores, banks, offices, newspapers, moving-picture theaters, hotels, restaurants, and service shops. Buildings in this area are of brick or stone and for the most part from three to six stories in height. There is a tendency for stores such as clothing stores to offer a larger proportion of relatively low-priced merchandise than would be true in some cities of similar size as a result of the low buying power of a considerable fraction of the population. Hotel facilities seem below the average for cities of similar numbers; the city is not one attractive to tourists, and businessmen in these days of rapid transportation find the distance to Boston short.

This major retail trade district merges into districts of less concentration in which one-story shops, or taller buildings in which the lower floors are used for shops and the upper stories for residence, or, in most cases, a mixture of the two prevail. Retail shops of the same kinds as those in the major retail area are in general of lower quality or smaller size or both. Automobile filling stations, garages, repair shops, and salesrooms introduce into these districts an element not present in the more concentrated retail area. Lodginghouses replace hotels, and banks and offices disappear from the picture. Wooden buildings mingle with those of more substantial materials and in some districts prevail. Farther from the central district, buildings used entirely for residence appear among those used wholly or partly for business. Settlement of this type lines for many blocks some of the major thoroughfares.

Apart from the major district of retail trade, there are few areas which can be classed as commercial areas, since in most regions trade is mingled with either residence or manufacturing. South of the chief retail trade district is an area on Market and Middle Streets (Map III) in which retail trade, wholesale trade, and some kinds of manufacturing (printing, paper ruling, sign manufacture, medicine manufacture, sheet-metal work) are mingled. The establishments of plumbers and electrical contractors, dealers in mill supplies, wholesale dealers in meats, fruits, and liquors replace in part the types of retail shops common to the other areas described. Farther west, in the area between Broadway and the western part of the Pawtucket Canal, warehouses and concerns selling wholesale meats and produce, hay and grain, lumber, machinery, and mill supplies are mingled with manufacturing establishments. In the southern part of the city between River Meadow Brook and the New York, New Haven, and Hartford Railroad a considerable area is occupied by dealers in coal and oil, iron and steel, building materials, waste paper, and junk, together with several factories.

Near the outskirts of the city in the southern and northwestern sections much land is used for cemeteries, for hospitals, and for the city water works. Open areas bordering the Concord River, the Merrimack River, and the Pawtucket Canal are in large part the property of the Wamesit Power Company or the Proprietors of Locks and Canals.

The pattern which has been described is dependent in part upon the natural features of the city's site and the circumstances of its settlement and growth.

CHAPTER 3

The Evolution of the Pattern

The Central Industrial Area

THE FIRST cotton mill on the Merrimack River
on the site of the present city of Lowell began operations in 1823.[1] It was established by the Merrimack
Manufacturing Company, one of the two companies
now manufacturing cotton cloth in Lowell. Its pred-
ecessor, the Boston Manufacturing Company, had
begun cotton manufacture in 1814 in Waltham,[2]
putting into use for the first time in America a power
loom,[3] and operating the first factory in which all
the processes from the raw cotton to the finished
cloth were completed in a single mill.[4] This enterprise had flourished to such an extent that the directors of the company sought an opportunity to en-
large their industry beyond the limits set by the
small extent of the power of the Charles River at
Waltham. A site on the Merrimack River in what
was then the town of Chelmsford was determined

---

[1] S. A. Drake, *History of Middlesex County* (Boston: Estes and
Lauriat, 1880), II, 62.

[2] *Ibid.*, I, 184; II, 57.

[3] Nathan Appleton, *Introduction of the Power Loom and the Origin
of Lowell* (Lowell: B. H. Penhallow, 1858), pp. 8–9.

[4] *Ibid.*, p. 14.

upon, and the company, reorganized as The Merrimack Manufacturing Company, began the manufacture of cloth at its present location in 1823.[1]

Factors influencing the choice of Chelmsford as the site for the new factory were the extent of the water power available, the ease with which it could be developed, nearness to the port of Boston, and water connection with Boston already established by way of the Middlesex Canal. The Merrimack River in the forty-eight miles of its course between the New Hampshire boundary and the sea drops ninety feet;[2] a little more than one-third of the total fall occurred, before the location of dams on the river, within a distance of about one mile at Pawtucket Falls, nine miles south of the New Hampshire boundary. It was this falls which was chosen to provide the power for the new enterprise. The river has a mean discharge of 8,020 second-feet,[3] producing in a descent of 30 feet a theoretical motive force equivalent to about 27,000 horsepower.[4]

Years before the establishment of the Merrimack Manufacturing Company in Chelmsford, shipbuilders at Newburyport, at the mouth of the Merrimack,

---

[1] Drake, *op. cit.*, II, 58–62.

[2] U. S. Census Office, *Tenth Census of the United States: 1880*, Vol. XVI (Washington: Government Printing Office, 1885), p. 24.

[3] Computed from annual discharge averages, based on records kept by Proprietors of Locks and Canals, 1848–1915. U. S. Geological Survey, *Water Supply and Irrigation Paper 415* (Washington: Government Printing Office, 1916), pp. 227–33.

[4] One second-foot equals .1136 theoretical horsepower per foot of fall. *Ibid.*, p. 301.

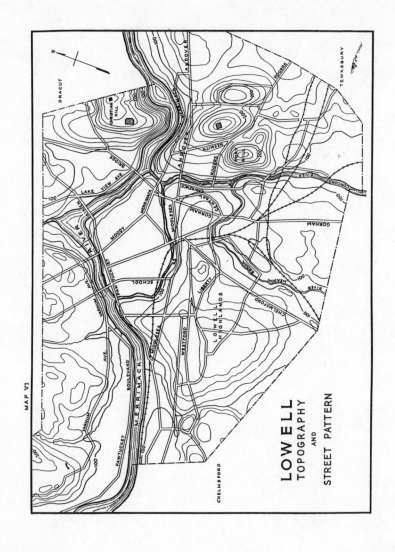

MAP VI

LOWELL
TOPOGRAPHY
AND
STREET PATTERN

had found Pawtucket Falls a serious obstacle in obtaining supplies of timber by way of the river from
the upper Merrimack country.[1] To lessen this handicap, the Pawtucket Canal was constructed and was
first opened for use in 1796.[2] It extended from a
point on the south bank of the river just above the
falls for a distance of a mile and a half southward
and eastward, joining the Concord River about one
thousand feet above the junction of this stream with
the Merrimack (Map. VI).[3] The descent in this distance was accomplished by means of four sets of
locks.[4] For a time the canal served the purpose for
which it was constructed, but its owners were des-
tined within a few years to have their hopes for
prosperity doomed by the construction of the
Middlesex Canal.

The Middlesex Canal was conceived as one link
in a comprehensive scheme to make large parts of
New Hampshire and Vermont tributary to the port
of Boston.[5] The construction of this canal connecting Boston with the Merrimack was to be followed
by extensive improvements on the river above the
head of the canal and by the development eventually
of connections between the Merrimack and the Con-

---

[1] Frank P. Hill, *Lowell Illustrated* (Lowell: Huse, Goodwin and
Co., 1884), p. 66.

[2] Drake, *op. cit.*, II, 53–54.

[3] Hill, *op. cit.*, p. 56.

[4] Drake, *op. cit.*, II, 54.

[5] M. W. Mann, "The Middlesex Canal, an Eighteenth Century Enterprise," *Boston Society Publications*, Vol. VI (Boston, 1910), pp. 70, 76.

necticut.[1] The canal was completed in 1804.[2] From
a junction with the Merrimack a mile above Pawtucket Falls it extended through Chelmsford, Billerica, Wilmington, Woburn, and Medford to a
southern terminus at the Charles River in Charlestown.[3] It was the first canal in the United States to
transport both passengers and merchandise.[4] The
canal was thirty-one miles long,[5] whereas it was forty
miles from the head of the canal by way of the river
to Newburyport. It was natural that the Middlesex
Canal, leaving the Merrimack a mile farther upstream, should divert to Charlestown much of the
ship timber which the Pawtucket Canal had been
designed to carry toward Newburyport.

The Pawtucket Canal, never a very profitable enterprise,[6] was financially ruined and, when the directors of the Boston Manufacturing Company in 1821
were looking for a water power, the capital stock of
the company owning this canal could be had for
little.[7] The directors bought it, as well as much land
between it and the river, and secured thereby entire

---

[1] J. L. Sullivan, *Remarks on the Importance of Inland Navigation
from Boston by Way of the Middlesex Canal and Merrimack River in
the Present and Probable Future State of Foreign Commerce* (Boston:
J. Eliot, 1813).

[2] Hill, *op. cit.,* p. 6.

[3] L. L. Dame, "The Middlesex Canal," *Old Residents Historical
Association of Lowell, Contributions* (Lowell, 1874–1904), III, 277.

[4] Charles Cowley, *Illustrated History of Lowell* (Boston: Lee and
Shephard, 1868), p. 27.

[5] Drake, *op. cit.,* II, 54.

[6] Appleton, *op. cit.,* p. 23.

[7] Hill, *op. cit.,* p. 66; Appleton, *op. cit.,* p. 23.

control of the power of Pawtucket Falls as well as a canal ready built to facilitate its use.[1]

Conditions for the ready utilization of the power were made still more favorable by the fact that the river here, shortly above the falls, makes a pronounced bend to the north, and below the falls bends again southward; the canal cuts across the base of the loop, inclosing between the river on the north and the canal on the south an area more than a mile square, much of which was suitable for the location of mills. By the construction of a low dam at the head of the falls, the enlargement of the old canal, and the building of branch canals, the power was made available with an expenditure relatively small in proportion to the gain.[2]

The Merrimack Company soon put two additional factories into operation and established a machine shop and print works.[3] By 1826 the company was making 2,000,000 yards of cotton cloth per year and nearly 1,000 employees were housed in the tenements erected for their operatives.[4] The success of this company stimulated the foundation of others. The Hamilton Manufacturing Company began the construction of cotton mills in 1825.[5] By the following year there was a manufacturing settlement of 2,500 pop-

---

[1] Drake, *op. cit.*, II, 62; H. A. Miles, *Lowell as It Was and as It Is* (Lowell, 1845), p. 27.

[2] Drake, *op. cit.*, II, 62.

[3] *Ibid.*, p. 63.

[4] *Ibid.*, p. 64.

[5] *Ibid.*, p. 63.

ulation [1] where there had been perhaps a dozen
houses in 1822.[2] This industrial portion of the town
then petitioned for separation from the remainder of
Chelmsford, and in 1826 a new town was incorporated.[3] It was called "Lowell" in honor of Francis
Cabot Lowell, who had introduced the power loom
in the factory of the Boston Manufacturing Company at Waltham and had thus laid the first of the
foundation stones upon which was based the prosperity of the new settlement.

It is obvious that the sites along the Merrimack
in Lowell suitable for the utilization of water power
are those below the rapids, but above the mouth of
the Concord, since the Pawtucket Canal discharges
into the Concord. Other possible sites for mills utilizing power are along the eastern portion of the
Pawtucket Canal, where mills may receive water by
means of a branch canal from a higher level of the
main canal and discharge into it at a lower level, or
receive from the lower level and discharge into the
Concord. The site chosen for the Merrimack Company was on the river at the foot of the present Dutton Street, where practically the full fall could be
utilized; that for the Hamilton Company, on the
south side of the lower Pawtucket Canal just west
of the present Central Street (Map VII). The
branch canals serving the two mills are those follow-

---

[1] Miles, *op. cit.,* p. 40.
[2] Appleton, *op. cit.,* p. 19.
[3] Drake, *op. cit.,* II, 63, 64.

MAP VII

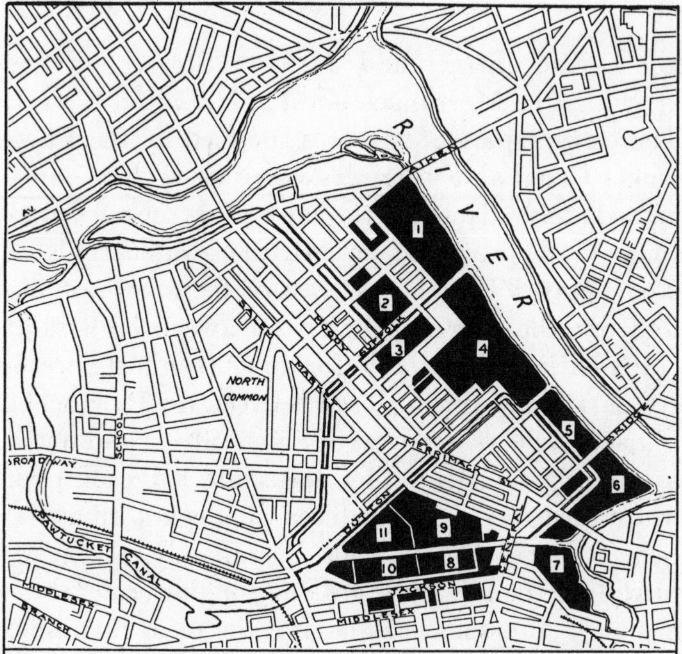

AREAS OCCUPIED IN 1912 BY THE CORPORATIONS
IN LOWELL USING MERRIMACK POWER

1. LAWRENCE MANUFACTURING COMPANY
2. SUFFOLK MILLS
3. TREMONT MILLS
4. MERRIMACK MANUFACTURING COMPANY
5. BOOTT MILLS
6. MASSACHUSETTS COTTON MILLS
7. MIDDLESEX COMPANY
8. HAMILTON MANUFACTURING COMPANY
9. BIGELOW CARPET COMPANY
10. APPLETON COMPANY
11. LOWELL MACHINE SHOP

0'   1200'   2400'

ing Dutton Street and Jackson Street and are known as the Merrimack and the Hamilton Canals. The eastern part of the area inclosed by the Pawtucket Canal and the rivers, together with the area immediately adjoining the lower Pawtucket Canal on the south, provides a broad expanse of nearly level land (Map VI), whereas east of the mouth of the Concord the Merrimack flows between high sand bluffs entirely unsuitable for mill sites; in the western part of the area inclosed between the Pawtucket Canal and the rivers, west of Salem Street and north of Broadway (Map II), the same ledge of rock which forms the falls produces what is known as the School Street Hill.[1] Thus, fortunately, the areas providing the locations suitable for power development are also the areas having the most favorable topography for the construction of mills.

As additional mills were added, they occupied the areas east and west of the Merrimack Company along and near the river front, east and west of the Hamilton mills along the Pawtucket Canal, and the angle between the Pawtucket and Merrimack Canals (Map VII). These mills appeared in rapid

---

[1] The U. S. G. S. topographic map, upon which Map VI is based, is clearly inaccurate in this School Street area. No hill is indicated by the contours, whereas the hill is actually a conspicuous topographic feature which should appear with a contour interval of 20 feet. There are insufficient data available for correcting the map, but figures showing street grade along School Street, recorded in the City Engineer's Office, indicate a rise of 53 feet between a point at the intersection of School Street and Broadway and a point on School Street about 1,100 feet farther north, which is the approximate summit of the hill.

succession. The Appleton Company was organized
for cotton manufacture in 1828.[1] The Lowell Manufacturing Company, also founded in 1828, engaged
partly in cotton manufacture but began also the
production of Brussels carpet.[2] This beginning of
woolen manufacture was followed by the establishment in 1830 of the Middlesex Company as makers
of broadcloths, cashmeres, and other woolen cloth.[3]
The Suffolk Manufacturing Company, the Tremont Mills, and the Lawrence Manufacturing
Company were all incorporated for cotton manufacture in 1831.[4] The Western (Suffolk Street) Canal
was constructed to supply water for this group of
factories. Soon after, the Eastern Canal (along
Canal Street, Map III) was completed to serve the
Boott Cotton Mills, established in 1835,[5] and the
Massachusetts Cotton Mills, tenth and last of the
great textile corporations using Merrimack power,
which followed in 1839.[6]

In 1826 the Merrimack Company transferred to
an organization incorporated as the Proprietors of
Locks and Canals its machine shop and all the land
and water power which the corporation owned except sufficient for the operation of its own mills and
print works. The Proprietors of Locks and Canals,
in turn, provided land and power and, in most cases,
erected mills and manufactured all the machinery

[1] Hill, *op. cit.*, p. 75.　　[4] Drake, *op. cit.*, II, 68.
[2] *Ibid.*, p. 77.　　[5] *Ibid.*, p. 71.
[3] *Ibid.*, p. 79.　　[6] *Ibid.*, p. 76.

for the other corporations which were founded following the initial success of the Merrimack and Hamilton Companies.[1] When the last of the cotton companies had been added, the ten textile plants and the Locks and Canals machine shop formed a semicircle of mills extending eastward from the bend in the river, which is also the approximate base of the falls, to the mouth of the Concord, and from there southward and westward to the point where the Merrimack and Hamilton Canals diverge from the main canal. Except for the enlargement, in later years, of the plants of the various corporations on their own premises, the greater part of the central mill ring had thus been completed by 1840. Map VII shows that except for a change in the ownership of one of the textile plants the original corporations were still established on their original sites in 1912. It has been shown that the sites for the early mills were indicated by topography. It remained for the growing settlement developing around the industrial nucleus to accommodate itself to the pattern which was thus begun.

Such growth as Lowell experienced in the years following the incorporation of the town had been previously unequaled in American town history. The population rose from 2,500 in 1826 to 17,633 in 1836.[2] In that year Lowell became a city, the first on the Merrimack in Massachusetts. At the census

---

[1] Drake, *op. cit.,* II, 63.   [2] Miles, *op. cit.,* pp. 40–41.

of 1840, Lowell, with a population of 20,796, was the second city of the commonwealth.[1]

The Early Commercial Center

As the semicircle of textile mills developed and the population grew in response to growing industry, it was natural that a street extending east and west between the northern and the southern rows of mills, with their associated dwelling and lodginghouses, should become a major thoroughfare and that on this street should be centered much of the commercial life of the new settlement. The town directory for 1834 shows that Merrimack Street extended through the town from the Concord River, north bridge, westward to what was then the Chelmsford line, and that its eastern portion had become a focus of retail trade.[2] Commercial enterprises were already varied. Clothing, shoes, dry goods, silks, shawls, linens and laces, china and hardware, West India goods, groceries, confectionery, drugs, books, and "fancy goods" all were offered by the merchants of Merrimack Street.[3] Number 1 Merrimack Street, "two doors west of the post office," was the "Town House" in which several

[1] U. S. Census Office, *Eleventh Census of the United States: 1890,* Vol. I, *Population,* Part I (Washington: Government Printing Office, 1895), pp. 371, 373.

[2] Benjamin Floyd, *The Lowell Directory, 1834* (Lowell: The Observer Press, 1834), p. 131.

[3] *Ibid.,* "Lowell Annual Advertiser" (prefixed to *The Lowell Directory,* unpaged).

merchants were housed.[1] Number 2 Merrimack Street was at the corner of Merrimack and Central Streets.[2] Here "seasonable clothing" was offered, including such diverse items as "gentlemen's opera tippets," "oriental dressing gowns," and a full line of "India rubber garments." "Bleachers, and all others much exposed to wet" were urged to call.[3] Beyond Number 2, mercantile establishments appear to have continued westward at least as far as Number 55, which was "under the South Church." [4] Merrimac House, for many years a leading hostelry, was at the corner of Merrimack and Dutton Streets, and there were two additional "houses of entertainment" on Merrimack Street.[5]

To the growth of the young settlement northward beyond the mill ring, the Merrimack River constituted an obstacle. There was no barrier to its growth southward except the Pawtucket Canal, which was readily bridged. The mills themselves, however, occupied the space along the canal from Dutton Street to the Concord River except for the break between the Hamilton mills at the eastern end of the Hamilton Canal and the Middlesex mills on the Concord. Thus, there developed only two through north-south streets crossing the central and eastern portions of the canal. These were Thorndike Street; connecting with Dutton Street at the

---

[1] *Ibid.*
[2] *Ibid.*
[3] *Ibid.*
[4] *Ibid.*
[5] *Ibid.*, p. 149.

western end of the mills, and Central Street, extending from Merrimack Street southward through the break in the mill ring. Thorndike Street was on the western fringe of the settled area, whereas Central Street adjoined the commercial portion of Merrimack Street and passed through an area of concentrated settlement. It was natural therefore that commercial establishments were attracted to Central Street. In 1834 it had begun to take its place as a part of the commercial district. The American House and Washington Hotel were there,[1] and some shops occurred along it at least as far south as Jackson Street. There were few shops elsewhere. The commercial district was confined, as is the major district of retail trade today, almost entirely to the eastern portion of Merrimack and the northern part of Central Street. Shortly south of Jackson Street the land rises to form a low elevation known as Chapel Hill, and Central Street bent eastward skirting its base (Map VI).

An Early Civic Center

The early manufacturing companies were concerned for the material and spiritual welfare of their operatives. They built substantial lodginghouses in which to house their workers and carefully supervised their social life. The Merrimack Company in 1824 built St. Anne's Church (Fig. 18) [2] to serve

---

[1] *Ibid.*   [2] Stone, *op. cit.,* p. 731.

their employees' spiritual needs. Placed conveniently near the Merrimack corporation houses on
Dutton Street, it stands at the intersection of Merrimack Street and the Merrimack Canal (Map III).
It marks today the western terminus of the major
retail district on the north side of Merrimack Street,
and, with the growth of the city, has become one focus
of civic, social, and educational development. Near
it are grouped the High School, the City Hall, the
Library, the Y. M. C. A., the Masonic Temple, and
another of the leading churches (Map III).

Early Distribution of Settlement

The town of Lowell, as incorporated in 1826,
was bounded on the north and east by the Merrimack
and Concord Rivers. The western and southern
boundaries were formed by a line extending from
the Merrimack two hundred rods above the head of
the Pawtucket Canal southward to the Middlesex
Canal, along this canal for twenty rods, thence eastward to the Concord.[1] Settlement in the early
thirties, except for a few houses on School Street
and on Pawtucket Street near the dam, was confined
to the eastern portion of the town, that is, to the area
within the mill semicircle and the area extending
southward from this between Thorndike Street and
the Concord River toward River Meadow Brook.[2]

---

[1] Drake, *op. cit.*, II, 53.
[2] Benjamin Mather, *Plan of the Town of Lowell and Belvidere Village, 1832* (map) ; Floyd, *op. cit.*

In this last area the greater part of the population was between Central Street and the Concord River. Large numbers of the population lived in the houses built by the corporations and adjoining the mills. Place of residence in the 1834 directory is indicated, in many cases, not by streets, but by corporations; "32 Hamilton corporation," "27 Appleton corporation," "2 Suffolk blocks," "22 Carpet blocks" are typical addresses. Besides the settlement within Lowell, population had spread eastward across the lower Concord into that portion of Tewksbury known as Belvidere (Map II).[1] In 1834 the western part of Belvidere was separated from Tewksbury and annexed to Lowell.[2]

The Concord Industrial Area

The extension of settlement along and across the Concord suggests that this stream too was not without importance in the town's early history. Most of such manufacturing as had been done in eastern Chelmsford before the founding of the Merrimack Manufacturing Company had utilized the power of the Concord and of its tributary, River Meadow Brook, while the Merrimack had been used only to turn the wheels of an insignificant sawmill near the foot of Pawtucket Falls.[3] As early as 1790 Moses

---

[1] *Ibid.*
[2] Drake, *op. cit.*, II, 70.
[3] Drake, *op. cit.*, II, 56; J. W. Meader, *The Merrimack River* (Boston: B. B. Russel, 1869), p. 246.

Hale had a fulling mill at a dam on River Meadow
Brook about two hundred fifty feet below the present Gorham Street bridge.[1] Later he acquired more
land, added saw and grist mills, and operated what
is believed to have been the first carding machine in
Middlesex County.[2] In 1812 he built another dam
nearer the Concord on the same stream and in 1817
commenced the manufacture of gunpowder at the
lower dam.[3] This business was later continued by
Oliver Whipple, who enlarged it,[4] making use of the
larger water power provided by the falls of the
Concord just above the mouth of River Meadow
Brook, where the river falls about twenty-three feet.
This power he brought into use by the construction of a canal extending from the head of the falls
northward on the left side of and parallel to the
river, then bending westward and discharging into
River Meadow Brook.[5] This canal was constructed
in 1821 and is claimed to be the first in this country
developed for the purpose of power utilization.[6] In
1834 Whipple's powder works were still in operation and were producing 750,000 pounds of powder
yearly.[7] The Lowell Bleachery, which was to occupy

[1] A. Gilman, "Moses Hale, an Early Manufacturer of Wool," *Old
Residents Historical Association, Contributions,* I, 243-46.
[2] *Ibid.*
[3] *Ibid.*
[4] Sara S. Griffin, *Quaint Bits of Lowell History* (Lowell: Butterfield Co., 1913), p. 25.
[5] Meader, *op. cit.,* p. 264.
[6] *Ibid.*
[7] *Floyd, op. cit.,* p. 8.

a site on the River Meadow Brook near the western
end of the canal for almost the whole of a century,
was established in 1832.[1]

A falls lower on the Concord, near its mouth, was
also utilized before the founding of Lowell. The
fall at the dam constructed here is about twelve
feet.[2] A mill was erected here in 1813, just above
the junction of the Pawtucket Canal with the Concord River, and "this river supplied the power to
operate its machinery." [3] It appears to have been first
occupied by a versatile manufacturer who spun cotton yarn, carded wool, manufactured looms of his
own invention for weaving suspenders and boot-
straps, and made other machinery for cotton and
woolen manufacture.[4] It was sold in 1818 to Thomas
Hurd, who built an additional mill and converted
both into a woolen factory.[5] Hurd's mill was on the
site later occupied by the Middlesex Company and
became a part of its property when it was established in 1828.[6] When Lowell was incorporated
in 1826, there were also a flannel mill and a grist mill
opposite what is now the Middlesex property on the
eastern side of the river.[7] A flannel mill is mentioned in the 1834 directory in giving the occupa-

---

[1] *Ibid.*, p. 140.
[2] *Tenth Census of the United States: 1880*, XVI, 41.
[3] Miles, *op. cit.*, p. 18.
[4] Drake, *op. cit.*, II, 55.
[5] *Ibid.*
[6] *Ibid.*
[7] A. B. Wright, "Lowell in 1826," *Old Residents Historical Association, Contributions*, III, 428.

tions of residents of Belvidere and also a card factory which may have been in the same vicinity.[1]

Between the falls used by the Middlesex Company and that which supplied the power for Whipple's powder works there is a third low fall which
offers only an insignificant amount of power. Before the founding of Lowell this was the site of an
iron foundry[2] where hoes and shovels were manufactured and iron for machinery cast.[3]

Thus was initiated the industrial district bordering the Concord. Unlike the Merrimack mill ring,
which, after the founding of the ten original textile
corporations, except for the enlargement of the
plants of these companies, remained for the greater
part of a century almost unaltered, the Concord
mill groups experienced frequent changes. The far
smaller power of the Concord (about 1200 horsepower but varying with the season) attracted for
the most part smaller enterprises; the large plant
of the Middlesex Company, at the lowest fall on the
Concord, and also at the eastern terminus of the
Pawtucket Canal, used both Concord and Merrimack power. The smaller establishments showed
less stability than the large textile corporations on
the Merrimack. In 1848 there was a factory for
utilizing cotton waste at the middle fall on the site

---

[1] Floyd, *op. cit.,* pp. 155–57.

[2] *Handbook for the Visitor to Lowell* (Lowell: A. Watson, 1848),
p. 18.

[3] Wilkes Allen, *The History of Chelmsford* (Haverhill: P. N. Green,
1820), p. 41.

of the earlier iron foundry, while Whipple's canal
at the upper fall provided power for a grist mill, a
bobbin factory, and print works in addition to the
powder mill, and River Meadow Brook near by had
a paper mill and a small establishment making cotton carpets.[1] In 1880 there were a woolen mill and
several other small factories on the east side of the
river opposite the Middlesex mills, and at the middle fall a paper mill and a woolen mill.[2] The power
at the upper fall had come into the hands of the
Wamesit Power Company and other owners, including the Belvidere Woolen Company, the Stirling Woolen Mill, Faulkner and Son (woolen
manufacturers), a grist mill, and a bolt manufacturing company; the Wamesit Power Company
leased power to various small establishments.[3] In
1918 the Concord supplied power for the United
States Cartridge Company, which obtained power
through the Wamesit Power Company, for the
Lowell Bleachery, and for six woolen or worsted
mills. In addition, the Waterhead Mills, corduroy
converters, were established near the head of the
canal at the upper falls, using no power, but obtaining water for processing from the river.

It is apparent that, although companies came and
went and the character of manufacture changed,
land bordering each of the three falls on the Con-

---

[1] *Handbook for the Visitor to Lowell* (1848), pp. 18–19.
[2] *Tenth Census of the United States: 1880,* XVI, 41.
[3] *Ibid.*

cord was the site of one or more factories from the
earliest days of the town, and that woolen and
worsted manufacture became increasingly concentrated on these sites. Since the Merrimack power
sites had been mainly used by cotton manufacturing
companies, the areas near the falls of the Concord
were the only remaining sites in the city where
woolen manufacturers could obtain both power and
an adequate supply of soft water for washing, fulling, and dyeing. For the Lowell Bleachery also the
river supplied not only power but the necessary
process water. Before 1918 the middle fall, which
also was acquired by the Wamesit Power Company,
had ceased to be used for power because it furnished
too little permanent power to be considered worth
developing. Nevertheless the space between the
upper and the lower falls on the east side of the
river had come to be occupied by a continuous series
of factories. The supply of water for industrial
purposes other than power was one of the attrac-
tions which this area offered. Concord water is used
by the American Hide and Leather Company (Map
V) for processing and for boilers, and by the Lowell
Electric Light Corporation (Map V) for boilers
and for condenser cooling. Moreover, for all companies located in this area the branch railway line
which was extended along the east bank of the river,
then across it to a point opposite the Middlesex
mills (Map V), provided a convenient means of
transportation.

Thus the Concord industrial area gradually assumed its present shape. At the upper fall the power canal is on the left side of the river and the factories using power are confined to the left bank of the Concord and the lower reaches of River Meadow Brook. The abrupt slope of Fort Hill bordering the right bank of the river at the falls (Map VI) would apparently have prevented the construction of the power canal on the east side of the river and also the use of the east bank as the site for mills not dependent upon water power. As far south as topography permits begins the line of mills on the right bank following the railroad. At the lower falls, as has been shown, power has long been utilized on both sides of the river, though the greater part of the available power is owned by the Middlesex Company. In the course of the recent depression several companies established on the east bank opposite the Middlesex Company have ceased operations or moved elsewhere, and a company manufacturing paper boxes is the only one now remaining on the right side of the river at the Middlesex dam. Most of the small mill buildings clustered on this site were razed following the damage done by the great spring flood in 1936.

The Railroads and the Railroad Industrial Areas

When the water power of the Merrimack had been taken up by the large textile corporations and that of the Concord by the smaller establishments

which occupied its banks, further growth of manufacturing was dependent upon steam power. Except for such establishments as required a water
supply for industrial purposes other than power,
wide choice of location was open to the steam-driven
mills. After the construction of railroads, however,
sites along a railroad or near enough one to be
reached by short lateral spurs offered exceptional
advantages for transportation. It was natural
therefore that many of the industrial plants operated by steam should select railroad sites. Thus the
series of mills following the railroads slowly developed as the city and its industries grew.

The Boston and Lowell Railroad, one of the first
few in the United States, was completed in 1835.[1]
Before that date the chief raw materials for the
young town's thriving industries and most of the
finished products of its manufactures were hauled
to and from Boston by horses over wagon roads or
towed by oxen along the Middlesex Canal. Within
a few years after the opening of the railroad from
Boston, rail transportation was extended up the
Merrimack Valley to Nashua, New Hampshire, by
means of the Nashua and Lowell Railroad, completed in 1838.[2] The city of Nashua being on the
west side of the Merrimack, the railroad does not
cross the river in Lowell, but immediately north of
the station on Middlesex and Thorndike Streets

---

[1] Appleton, *op. cit.*, p. 36.   [2] Drake, *op. cit.*, II, 75.

(Map II) bends westward, and extends to the great bend of the river (Map I), thence northward along the right bank to Nashua. A branch line extending northward along Dutton Street serves the Merrimack group of industrial corporations (Map III).

Additional railroads soon followed. The decline of traffic on the Middlesex Canal following the opening of the first railroad left the transportation of freight to and from the city in large part in the hands of the Boston and Lowell Company. Differences between this company and one of Lowell's enterprising citizens whose business supplied a considerable tonnage to the road led to agitation for competing railways which resulted in the construction of two additional roads; the Lowell and Lawrence Railroad was completed in 1847,[1] and before the last boat on the Middlesex Canal was run in 1852[2] the Salem and Lowell Railroad had been completed.[3] These two roads leave Lowell as one, separating at Tewksbury junction six miles east of the city; one extends northward to Lawrence, the other southeastward to Salem. A road between Framingham and Lowell was opened for travel in 1871,[4] and the Lowell and Andover Railroad, ex-

---

[1] J. B. French, "William Livingston," *Old Residents Historical Association, Contributions,* I, 102.

[2] A. T. Hopkins, "The Old Middlesex Canal," *New England Magazine,* New Series XVII (January, 1898), 532.

[3] Hill, *op. cit.,* p. 11.

[4] *Ibid.,* p. 14.

tending eastward to Lowell Junction where it connects with the main line of the Boston and Maine from Boston to Lawrence, in 1874.[1] The Framingham and Lowell Railroad is now a part of the New York, New Haven, and Hartford system, while all the other roads are controlled by the Boston and Maine (Map II).

The topography of the city is such as to afford easy access to railroads from the south (Map VI). Between the Fort Hill drumlin on the east and a rock ledge which forms an abrupt elevation in the area inclosed by Liberty, Chelmsford, and Westford Streets on the west the topography offers little difficulty. The several railroads converge upon the city from the south, southeast, and southwest and unite as they pass through the broad gateway between these two elevations toward the terminal on Middlesex Street.

The development of the series of factories along and near the railroads has occupied the whole period of the city's growth since the coming of the first railway. One of the present establishments near the heart of town, for example, was founded in 1837, while the Imperial Upholstery Company, at the western margin of the city, was established in 1917. The area in which most of the earlier establishments were located was the area immediately adjoining the textile mill ring on the west, that is,

---

[1] *Ibid.,* p. 16.

the area south of Broadway and west of Dutton Street, bordering the Pawtucket Canal. This area, without the railroad, would have been a natural region for early industrial expansion because of its juxtaposition to the earlier industrial districts and the settled portion of the town, and, in contrast to the area north of Broadway, its favorable topography. The railroad contributed an additional factor which to some of the establishments founded in this region, notably the gas company (Map V), first organized in 1849, and several lumber and woodworking companies, was an undoubted advantage.

Among the early industries using steam power, sawmills and planing mills held a place of importance.[1] The rapid growth of the town and the city in its early years must have provided a large market for their products. "In 1845, Mr. Norcross built a large lumber mill at Lowell, where with gangs of saws, upright and circular, he wrought out much of the lumber for the mills and dwellings of the city."[2] The Davis, Melandy, and Sargent Company, founded in 1840, operated a sawmill and later a planing mill and box factory.[3] William Livingston built a sawmill and a planing mill in 1848.[4] The A. L. Brooks Company founded a sawmill and lumber business as early as 1830.[5] The location of

---

[1] *Handbook for the Visitor to Lowell* (1848), pp. 42–43.
[2] Meader, *op. cit.*, p. 287.
[3] Stone, *op. cit.*, I, 743.
[4] French, *op. cit.*, p. 101.
[5] Stone, *op. cit.*, I, 737.

these early companies is not in all cases clear; Livingston's mill was at his wharf on the Middlesex Canal and the Davis, Melandy, and Sargent saw-mill was on the banks of the Pawtucket Canal. The concentration of the lumber business today in the area bordering the middle portion of the Pawtucket Canal suggests a survival from the period when New Hampshire timber arrived at Lowell by way of the Merrimack and entered the canal at the head of the falls.

Though much of the machine work for the corporations was done by the Locks and Canals machine shop, it was natural that in an industrial town other establishments should soon appear for the manufacture of foundry and machine-shop products and various mill supplies. A catalogue of steam manufactures in 1848 shows already established an iron foundry, "mechanics' mills," and makers of machinists' tools, bobbins, shuttles, cards, reeds, and pickers.[1] Companies now operating in the area near the canal between Broadway and Middlesex Street for the manufacture of machinery and machine parts, and for machine repair and other metal work, range in date of foundation from 1837 to recent years but were for the most part established before 1890.

Other industries are more recent additions to this area. The Massachusetts Mohair Plush Company,

---

[1] *Handbook for the Visitor to Lowell* (1848), pp. 42–43.

on the canal west of Thorndike Street, was established there in 1892. To this company the site offers access to canal water for processing as well as to rail facilities. Of the shoe companies now manufacturing in Lowell, the two in this district were the first two established. One of them was located there in 1903, while the other built its present factory, near Broadway just west of the canal, in 1892.

The southern portion of the railway industrial belt originated somewhat later than the central portion, though not later than the more recent additions to the central district. For example, the boilerworks in the region near River Meadow Brook was founded in 1879, the brewery in the same region in 1898, the fertilizer factory at the southern margin of the city in 1895. Since the area between the railroad and River Meadow Brook has remained a little-settled area, it continues to provide satisfactory sites for such establishments as the boilerworks and the principal iron foundry. The advantage of the location chosen for the fertilizer factory is its position beyond the margin of settlement. The brewery obtains the water used in manufacture from wells on the company's grounds, and the availability of an excellent water supply at this site was a major factor in its choice of location. In the western portion of the railway industrial area, factories were constructed at various dates in accordance with the areal expansion of the city.

Expansion of the Residential Districts

It has been shown that in the early 1830's settlement in Lowell was almost wholly confined to the eastern portion of the area inclosed between the Pawtucket Canal and the Merrimack River and to the district south of this bordering the Concord. The areas soon to be occupied by the Boott and Massachusetts Mills were for the most part vacant. The Merrimack was bridged on the approximate sites of the present Central Bridge (Bridge Street) and Pawtucket Bridge (School Street), but the areas at the southern ends of these bridges were sparsely settled or vacant and there had been no movement across the river onto the Dracut side.[1]

By 1850 the present principal streets had appeared in the western part of the area between the canal and the river and there was some settlement, though scattered, in that area.[2] The triangle between the river and Merrimack Street west of the Lawrence Company and the Suffolk Mills (Map VII), the "Little Canada" of later years, was almost vacant.[3] North and South Commons had been laid out and there was close settlement between the South Common and the Concord, south to River Meadow Brook.[4] Following the railroad, settlement had extended along Middlesex Street as far

---

[1] Mather, *op. cit.*
[2] Sidney and Neff, *Plan of the City of Lowell in 1850.*
[3] *Ibid.*
[4] *Ibid.*

west as School Street. Population had crossed Central Bridge and occupied a considerable area in Centralville.[1] In 1851 Centralville was detached from Dracut and annexed to Lowell.[2] It contained some nine hundred people at the time of annexation.[3]

By 1876 the district of the School Street Hill was well occupied and the southern part of Little Canada filled.[4] Settlement had spread northward and westward in Centralville, eastward in Belvidere, and westward and southward in the part of the city south of the Pawtucket Canal. The Aiken Street and Moody Street bridges had not yet been constructed and wooded areas bordered the north bank of the Merrimack near the bend. The area of the city had been greatly enlarged in 1874 by the accession of additional territory from Dracut (Pawtucketville section), Tewksbury, and Chelmsford.[5] The territory annexed from Chelmsford consisted of 1,000 acres, including Middlesex Village, the settlement which had developed near the head of the Middlesex Canal, and much of the Highlands district; it was estimated to contain only 216 inhabi-

---

[1] *Ibid.*

[2] Lowell Board of Trade, *Digest of the City of Lowell and Surrounding Towns* (Lowell, 1916), p. 26.

[3] Drake, *op. cit.*, II, 86.

[4] *Birds-eye View of Lowell, Lawrence and Other Cities* (Boston: O. H. Bailey and Co., 1876).

[5] Commonwealth of Massachusetts, Harbor and Land Commission, *Atlas of the Boundaries of the City of Lowell and the Towns of Ayer, Billerica, Carlisle, Chelmsford, Dracut, Dunstable, etc.*, 1907.

tants at the time of annexation.[1] Pawtucketville
is not shown on the map of 1876. By 1879 there had
been a movement of population into this area;
Mammoth Road (the extension of School Street
north of the river) had appeared and some of the
streets east of this.[2] Additional territory in Pawtucketville was annexed in 1879.[3]

In 1883 the Merrimack was bridged at Aiken
Street, and the Moody Street bridge was constructed in 1894. Spread of settlement in Centralville and Pawtucketville north of these bridges followed. Settlement is still very sparse in the north
central area to either side of Beaver Brook (the
stream entering the Merrimack from the north at
the bend), and in the northwestern section of the
city between Pawtucket Boulevard and Varnum
Avenue. Further additions of territory from
Tewksbury in the eastern and southeastern sections
of the city were made in 1888 and 1906.[4] The most
recent extensions of occupation have been in these
districts and in the western and southern fringes of
the Highlands.

The growth described was, in general, the radial
expansion to be expected in a region without very
serious topographic barriers. Extension to the
north was delayed as compared with growth south-

---

[1] Drake, *op. cit.*, II, 97 (Date of annexation is here given as 1873).
[2] G. M. Hopkins, *City Atlas of Lowell* (Philadelphia, 1879).
[3] Lowell Board of Trade, *op. cit.*, p. 26.
[4] *Ibid.*

ward, awaiting the construction of bridges. The
steeply sloping hill district in Belvidere, consisting
of a cluster of drumlins (Map VI), was occupied
late, whereas growth westward over the gentle
slopes of the Highlands area was more rapid. Settlement spread southward onto the nearly level
lands along the Concord earlier than it ascended the
abrupt southern slope of the School Street Hill.
The very steep south-facing slope of Christian Hill
is without settlement. Low, damp lands along the
upper reaches of the Concord above the falls and
along River Meadow Brook and Beaver Brook remain in large part unoccupied.

Areal expansion of course accompanied growth
in population. The population doubled between
1840 and 1870 (1840—20,796;[1] 1870—40,928[2]), a
serious recession having been experienced in the
war years, 1860 to 1865. It doubled again between
1870 and 1895 (84,367).[3] It rose to 112,759 in
1920, after which the recent recession began.

It was in the periods of growth following 1840
that the city came to have so large a foreign population. In the early years of Lowell's industrial development the mill operatives were recruited from
local sources. They were chiefly the daughters and

---

[1] *Eleventh Census of the United States: 1890,* Vol. I, *Population,*
Part I, p. 371.

[2] U. S. Census Office, *Ninth Census of the United States: 1870,* Vol.
I, *Population* (Washington: Government Printing Office, 1872), p. 166.

[3] Commonwealth of Massachusetts, Bureau of Statistics of Labor,
Census of Massachusetts, 1895, I, 50,

sons of New England farmers, attracted to the mills by the steady wages, the relatively low cost of living made possible by the careful provisions of the corporations for the housing and boarding of their workers, and by the remarkably favorable social conditions which were then maintained among the factory employees.[1] As late as 1847 more than five-sixths of the women employed in the Lowell mills were of New England birth.[2]

As the country's industry developed and new opportunities were offered to labor, men and women of American birth passed gradually into employments requiring more individual skill or into occupations easier or better paid.[3] Their places were taken in large part by Irish laborers who had made initial settlements in Lowell before 1833 and who came in great numbers in the years of Irish famine.[4]

During both the American and the Irish period, English and Scotch workers were present in lesser numbers. The introduction of calico printing in the Merrimack Company's mills in 1826 brought a small colony of skilled printers from Lancashire; workers from Renfrewshire, Scotland, appeared when ingrain carpet manufacture was undertaken

---

[1] Lillian W. Betts, "Lowell, the City of Spindles," *The Outlook,* LXIX (Oct. 12, 1901), 373–78.

[2] "Lowell and Its Manufactures," *The Merchants Magazine and Commercial Review,* XVI (April, 1847), 360.

[3] *Tenth Census of the United States: 1880,* Vol. II, *Manufactures* (Washington: Government Printing Office, 1883), p. 10.

[4] G. F. Kengott, *The Record of a City* (New York: The Macmillan Co., 1912), p. 29.

by the Lowell Corporation; and a colony from Gloucester was established in 1837 following the failure of a large firm in England.[1]

As the opening of new lands in the West caused a migration which left many New England farms deserted, some of these deserted lands were taken up by Irish settlers.[2] The places of the Irish in the mills came to be taken in part by French Canadians of whom there was a great influx in the period following the Civil War.[3] It was in this era of Canadian immigration that the area of Little Canada, previously little settled, came to be densely occupied. By 1900 Lowell had approximately 23,000 French Canadians.[4]

Though French Canadians and Irish still constitute the largest two foreign elements in the population, labor after 1890 was supplied increasingly by Greeks, Poles, Russians, Lithuanians, Italians, Portuguese, and people of other nationalities brought in by the flood of migration from southern and eastern Europe.[5]

Attracted by the mills, the immigrants in general

---

[1] Charles Cowley, "Foreign Colonies of Lowell," *Old Residents Historical Association, Contributions*, II, 168–74.

[2] *Tenth Census of the United States: 1880*, Vol. II, *Manufactures*, p. 10.

[3] Kengott, *op. cit.*, p. 29.

[4] U. S. Census Office, *Twelfth Census of the United States: 1900*, Vol. I, *Population*, Part I (Washington: U. S. Census Office, 1901), pp. 878, 882, 890, 898, 902. The figure given includes all those of French Canadian parentage.

[5] Kengott, *op. cit.*, pp. 28–32; *Fifteenth Census of the United States: 1930. Population*, Vol. II, pp. 248–50, 323.

occupied the more central areas of the city near the factories, while the native population moved to the outer districts. With the substitution of foreign for native labor it became impractical for the corporations to maintain the system of lodginghouses, boardinghouses, and company-owned residences previously operated. The immigrant populations were intolerant of social restrictions and preferred the greater freedom, though in many cases far poorer quarters, offered by other tenements. The corporation "blocks" were gradually abandoned by the corporations and many of them have lately been destroyed. As the textile companies enlarged their operations and the numbers employed in the mills increased, the necessity that the mill workers should live within a short distance of the mills resulted in high property values in the central part of the city, in overcrowding, in the construction of huge four-story wooden tenement blocks housing many families in small space, and in rapid and often flimsy building. Later, as improved methods of transportation made it possible for the mill workers to live at much greater distances from the mills, the spread of the laboring population into the outer areas began, and various districts of cottages or of smaller apartment buildings providing greater comfort and more access to light and air than were offered by the crowded tenements of the central areas gradually developed in regions removed from the central portion of the city.

The present residence pattern shows the combined effects of adjustment to topography and to industrial distribution. The better residential districts tend to occupy the hills and the poorer ones the lowlands. Fort Hill is reserved for a park, but the two drumlins east of Nesmith Street in Belvidere (Map VI) constitute a superior residence district (Fig. 14). Some beautiful and some pretentious homes crown their summits. West of Nesmith Street, as the land slopes downward and the mills are approached, settlement grades gradually into the low-medium or poor quality of residence found in the lowlands bordering the Concord. Also the lowlands south of Rogers Street, though removed from the mills, support only a medium or low-medium quality of settlement. Andover Street, extending for much of its length along or near the crest of the bluff bordering the Merrimack and commanding at some points a fine view of the river and the opposing bluffs, is lined with pleasant homes from Nesmith Street eastward (Map VI; Fig. 15).

Christian Hill in Centralville offers attractive sites for homes; however, the part of it near the Central Bridge is conveniently near the mills on the south bank of the Merrimack. Thus a poor residential district not only occupies the lowland to the west of Bridge Street but spreads east of it up the southwestern slopes of the hill. Farther north and east the Christian Hill area is one of good or high-intermediate quality and there is a conspicuous con-

trast between the high side and the low side of
Bridge Street. Quality of residence in the School
Street Hill area grades from low intermediate near
the base of its southern slope to high intermediate
and good in the higher lands nearer the river. The
hill district stands out in contrast to the poor areas
which occupy the lower lands to south and east.
Similarly, the hill in the triangle between Chelmsford, Liberty, and Westford Streets (Map VI)
constitutes an island of high-intermediate quality
surrounded by poorer districts.

The tongue of higher land extending eastward
from Chelmsford Street, between Middlesex Street
and River Meadow Brook (Map VI), was once
occupied by a residential district of high quality.
The Middlesex County Courthouse is located here,
also St. John's Episcopal Church, and other
churches. The nearness of the area to the mill districts has resulted in the occupation of much of it
by tenements and a population of foreign origin.

It has been seen that the section known as the
Highlands includes a residential district of high
quality (Figs. 16, 17). The area is in fact much
less a highland than the hills of Belvidere and Centralville (Map VI), but the western portion is well
removed from the mill districts. Quality declines
eastward.

The north bank of the Merrimack in the western
part of the city is bordered by nearly flat land, little
above the level of the river and subject to danger

from floods. Occupied areas are chiefly removed
from the river on and near Varnum Avenue and
though far from the mill districts do not constitute
residential districts of high quality. From near the
dam to the Moody Street bridge, the avenue bordering the river is farther above water level, commands a view of the falls, and is lined with attractive homes.

The Street Pattern

Direct adjustments to topography, as well as adjustments to the industrial pattern, which in turn is
related to topography, are apparent in Lowell's
street pattern. In the central part of the city within
the semicircle formed by the original textile mills,
the streets for the most part extend parallel to the
canals or at right angles to the canals and parallel
to the fronts of the mills which border the Merrimack River (Map II). The canals were obviously
constructed to enter the river at right angles. The
rectangular pattern of the streets suggests the approximate flatness of the surface. The convergence
of the Pawtucket Canal and the Merrimack River
introduces irregularity into the eastern portion of
the area; Merrimack Street must bend if it is to
pass north of the southern series of mills which
flanks the Pawtucket Canal. In the School Street
Hill area and the adjoining area between the Pawtucket Canal and Broadway, the street pattern is
influenced by the direction of the river and the

course of the Pawtucket Canal. Major streets are laid out to parallel one or the other of these waterways or to cross them approximately at right angles; minor streets are adjusted to the pattern thus begun.

In the areas beyond the central district (Map VI), the courses of East Merrimack Street, Lake View Avenue, Varnum Avenue, and its northward continuation, Riverside Street, Pawtucket Boulevard, Pawtucket Street, the western part of Middlesex Street, Chelmsford Street, and Lawrence Street are obviously planned to extend roughly parallel to the Merrimack River, Beaver Brook, River Meadow Brook, or the Concord River; while School, Moody, Aiken, and Bridge Streets cross the Merrimack at approximate right angles as they radiate from the central section of the city. The directions of various streets near the lower portion of River Meadow Brook are clearly adjusted to its course.

Andover Street east of Nesmith Street is directed along a belt of high ground south of the Merrimack between the Belvidere drumlins and the river bluff. The southern part of Gorham Street follows the divide between the Concord and River Meadow Brook. Nesmith Street and Rogers Street unite to pass through the gap between Fort Hill and the middle drumlin, while the streets east of Nesmith Street shown on Map VI are similarly adjusted to the contours. The Lowell and Lawrence Boulevard (not shown on Map VI) hugs the river at the foot of the south slope of Christian Hill, while Bridge Street skirts its western base. The course of Liberty Street appears to be affected by the rock ledge outcropping to form the hill on Chelmsford Street, and Central Street, as previously noted, conforms roughly to the contour of Chapel Hill. The directions of these streets whose courses are adjusted to the topographic pattern are diverse, and the streets which dissect the areas between these divergent arteries hence form, in various districts, an irregular and complicated net.

Other Features of the Pattern

As the street network was gradually extended with the city's growth, commercial areas as well as residence districts, of course, expanded. The radial growth of the city left the original commercial district on Merrimack and Central Streets in a focal position and it remained the major area of retail trade. Bridge Street, the northern part of Central Street, and Gorham Street together constitute the chief north-south artery through the city; hence the intersection of Merrimack Street and Central Street forms a natural commercial center. Commercial areas of less concentration including the smaller and lower-grade stores naturally developed in adjoining regions. Various foreign shops serving the foreign population of the central district are within these areas. To serve areas beyond the central nucleus, commercial settlement extended in tongues along

principal thoroughfares and in the areas north of
the river became concentrated at the bridge heads
(Map II). Of all the streets classed with the secondary commercial areas, Middlesex Street, bordering the central mill district on the south, most
nearly approaches Merrimack Street in quality.

Wholesale commercial establishments congregate
near railroads; Market and Middle Streets are
reached by a spur from the Dutton Street tracks
(Map III), while the other areas of wholesale trade
(p. 57) border principal railroad lines. Merchants
handling meat and produce choose the areas nearer
the district of retail trade, while dealers in coal and
oil, whose establishments are unsightly and occupy
considerable space, are relegated to the sparsely
settled area near River Meadow Brook.

It has been shown that a civic center developed
on Merrimack Street at the western end of the
major district of retail trade. With the destruction
of buildings bordering Merrimack Street, belonging to the Massachusetts Mills, a second civic center
has arisen at the eastern end of the chief commercial area. The new post office is here and just across
the Concord the public auditorium (Map III). A
hospital, a convent, and churches occupy an adjoining area. Other institutional property is widely
scattered.

Areas reserved for parks and playgrounds appear to be selected in part to give relief in the most
congested districts, as in the cases of North and
South Commons, in part to utilize space available

in sparsely settled regions, as illustrated by reservations in northeastern Centralville. Topography was undoubtedly a factor in the choice of Fort Hill as a park and, perhaps, in the placing of South Common, which occupies a somewhat depressed area surrounded by higher land. Cemeteries, though concentrated in the southeastern portion of the city near the Concord River, avoid the low wet areas along its banks.

Large areas owned by the city along the western part of Pawtucket Boulevard and between Chelmsford Street and River Meadow Brook are the sites of wells which supply the city's water. The Merrimack River was used as the source of the public water supply from 1870 until 1892. With increasing pollution of the river from upstream sources, the filtering system proved inadequate and the use of underground water was begun. Additional wells were later sunk and the use of river water was abandoned in 1897. Water is pumped to a main reservoir on Christian Hill and to a high service reservoir on a higher part of the same hill (Map VI). The Proprietors of Locks and Canals maintain a reservoir at the summit of a drumlin in Belvidere (Map VI) for fire protection in the mills and for other emergency needs.

Recent Changes in the Industrial Pattern

Throughout the period of expansion which has been described, the large textile corporations continued to constitute the primary basis for the city's

prosperity and, at least until 1890, were in large
part responsible for its growth. The Massachusetts
Mills, upon their establishment in 1839, leased the
last of the water power which the Proprietors of
Locks and Canals had for disposal.[1] In 1844 the
Prescott Company, subsequently consolidated with
the Massachusetts Mills,[2] filled a small gap in the
mill ring between Merrimack Street, the Pawtucket
Canal, and the Concord River, south of the Massachusetts Mills. Thereafter no other companies were
added to the central group except that in 1845 the
Lowell Machine Shop was organized as a corporation and took over the machine shops and foundry
previously operated by the Locks and Canals Company.[3] The Lowell Machine Shop and the textile
corporations using Merrimack power then bought
the stock of the Locks and Canals Company and
divided the available power among themselves in
proportion to their holdings,[4] thus becoming joint
proprietors rather than lessees of the power.[5]

Although there was no further power for sale the
owners were able to increase their operations in subsequent years by reason of improvements in the
system of power development and control and con-
sequent increased amounts of power available. This
increase was accomplished in part by the construc-

---

[1] Kengott, *op. cit.*, p. 7.
[2] Charles Cowley, *Illustrated History of Lowell*, p. 59.
[3] Drake, *op. cit.*, II, 79.
[4] Kengott, *op. cit.*, p. 7.
[5] Appleton, *op. cit.*, p. 35.

tion in 1846 of the Northern, or Grand, Canal,[1] which extends from the dam parallel to the south bank of the river, bends eastward to the Western Canal, connects by a subterranean feeder with the Merrimack Canal, and thus serves to maintain a fuller heàd of water in the distributing canals. Further, a new dam was constructed, the right to use higher flashboards was obtained, and some progress was made toward removing Hunt's Falls, a fall originally of eleven feet[2] about a mile below the city; by these means the height of the fall at Lowell was somewhat increased.[3] Partial control was secured of storage on a number of lakes in New Hampshire which supply water to Merrimack tributaries, and the regularity of flow of the main stream was thus improved.[4] As a result of improvements, the total range between tail water and full pond at Lowell was increased to 42 feet—though the average effective head is reduced to between 37 and 38 feet as a result of the drop along the canals and the limiting level at which water in the canals can be carried.[5] This means a total available power

---

[1] *Ibid.*

[2] Reduced to 7 or 8 feet partly by removal of reefs, partly by use of flashboards on the Lawrence dam. Commonwealth of Massachusetts, *Report of the Commission on Waterways and Public Lands on the Water Resources of Massachusetts,* Senate, No. 289 (Boston, 1918), p. 40.

[3] S. P. Hadley and Mabel Hill, "Lowell, a Character Sketch of the City," *New England Magazine,* New Series XIX (Jan., 1899), 643.

[4] *Tenth Census of the United States: 1880,* XVI, 29–30.

[5] Commonwealth of Massachusetts, *Report of the Commission on Waterways and Public Lands,* p. 40.

ranging between about 10,000 horsepower and
about 30,000 horsepower, when mills are operating
on the basis of 48 hours weekly.

The operations of the original manufacturing
companies were expanded not only by the use of the
increased water power but by the installation of
steam power. Engines for producing steam power
were installed in the Boott and Massachusetts plants
when they were constructed. Subsequently the earlier mills were similarly equipped, the Hamilton
Company installing steam equipment about 1850,
the Merrimack in 1856, and the Lawrence in 1871.
In 1880 the steam power installation in the nine [1]
textile corporations and the machine shop amounted
to 13,940 horsepower,[2] in 1918 to about 35,000
horsepower.

Growth of the textile corporations in accordance with the increase in power is indicated by
statistics of equipment, employment, and production. In 1839 the nine major textile corporations then operating had approximately 163,-
000 spindles and 5,000 looms, employed about 8,000
workers, and produced about 1,000,000 yards of
fabrics weekly.[3] In 1895 the same companies, with
the addition of the Massachusetts Mills, had about

---

[1] The original ten corporations reduced to nine by the consolidation
of Tremont and Suffolk, later separated again.

[2] *Tenth Census of the United States: 1880,* XVI, 33.

[3] James Montgomery, *The Cotton Manufacture of the United States
of America Compared and Contrasted with That of Great Britain*
(Glasgow: J. Niven, 1840), p. 160.

900,000 spindles and 26,000 looms, employed some
19,000 workers, and produced more than 6,500,000
yards of fabrics weekly.[1] The state census of 1895
shows 28,260 employed in all the industries of the
city.[2] It is thus apparent that in spite of the addition of many other companies and other industries,
the large textile corporations of the central industrial area were still responsible for a large fraction
of the city's industrial employment. After 1890,
numbers employed in the cotton and woolen and
worsted industries did not increase, although values
of products mounted. Figures for the individual
corporations are not available for 1918, the peak
year of the city's industries, but the cotton and
woolen industries for the city as a whole employed
17,148 workers in 1890, 13,964 in 1918, while values
of products soared from $23,251,538 in 1890 to
$73,593,623 in 1918.[3] Employment in these indus-
tries in 1923 was almost identical with that in 1918.

---

[1] Courier Citizen Company, *Illustrated History of Lowell* (Lowell,
1897), p. 287. The state census of 1895 shows figures for average employment which give a total of 19,209 for all the textile industries of the
city which are listed. Since part of the woolen, worsted, knit goods, and
dyeing industries were carried on at that time by companies not belonging to the group of corporations included in the Courier Citizen Company's figures, the figure of 19,000 for employment, though based upon
statistics from each company, is too high in relation to the census figure.
Possibly it represents maximum rather than average employment.

[2] Commonwealth of Massachusetts, Bureau of Statistics of Labor,
Census of Massachusetts, 1895, V, 600–601.

[3] *Eleventh Census of the United States: 1890,* Vol. VI, *Manufacturing Industries,* Part II (Washington: Government Printing Office,
1895), pp. 312–17; Commonwealth of Massachusetts, *Statistics of
Manufactures, 1918,* pp. 22–23.

Several changes occurred among the corporations of the inner ring after 1895. In 1896 the Lawrence Manufacturing Company discontinued cotton weaving and concentrated upon the manufacture of knitted cotton underwear and hosiery, which it had previously developed as a supplementary phase of manufacture. It continued its spinning department. The Lowell Manufacturing Company, which, from the beginning, combined cotton manufacture with the making of carpets, gave place to the Bigelow Carpet Company. In 1912 the Lowell Machine Shop was amalgamated with a machinery manufacturing company in Saco, Maine, to form the Saco-Lowell Shops. The Bigelow and Saco-Lowell companies continued operations in the plants of their predecessors, and no break was made in the long-established mill semicircle. Between 1912 and 1918, the Middlesex Company, the one company of the group making woolens, ceased to manufacture, and the Bigelow Carpet Company left the city, moving to Thompsonville, Connecticut, where there were other carpet factories. Lowell had been a pioneer in carpet manufacture, power looms for weaving woolen carpets having been first introduced by the inventor, Bigelow, in the mill of the Lowell Company in the 1840's,[1] and the removal of carpet manufacture was a serious loss to the city. The

[1] Samuel Fay, "Carpet Weaving and the Lowell Manufacturing Company," *Old Residents Historical Association, Contributions*, I, 52–61; Charles Cowley, *Illustrated History of Lowell*, p. 52.

mills, however, were soon occupied by the United States Cartridge Company, succeeded after the war by the Columbia Textile Company, dyers and finishers of cotton cloth, while the Middlesex Company's mills and power rights were sold to the Ipswich Mills, manufacturers of hosiery. The cotton companies continued intact. In 1923, one hundred years after the first wheel turned in the mills of the Merrimack Company, the original companies founded for cotton manufacture only were all operating on their original sites.

The year 1924 was a difficult one for the textile industries throughout the country after abnormally high production in 1923. In 1926, the centennial anniversary of its commencement of manufacturing, the Hamilton Company went into the hands of a receiver. Production was discontinued. This disaster initiated, within Lowell's central mill ring, a series of startling changes which followed in rapid succession during the four succeeding years. The Columbia Textile Company was liquidated. The Suffolk Mills were sold to the Nashua Manufacturing Company. The Tremont Mills were bought by the Merrimack Company and subsequently in large part destroyed. The Massachusetts Mills were sold to the Pepperell Manufacturing Company, which discontinued operations in Lowell soon after the purchase. The Appleton Company moved to Anderson, South Carolina. The Ipswich Mills sold out. Not only the textile mills but the Saco-Lowell

Shops were caught in the landslide; this company
consolidated its operations in Biddeford and Saco,
Maine, and the Lowell plant, which had supplied
textile machinery for many mills in this country and
abroad, had equipped the first cotton mill in China
and sent the first textile mill equipment to Brazil,
had constructed for the Boston and Lowell Railroad its first locomotive, and had turned the turrets
for the "Monitor," the first ironclad ship of the
United States Navy,[1] was razed shortly thereafter.
Of the eleven original corporations constituting the
mill ring only three remained—the Merrimack,
Boott, and Lawrence. The Nashua Manufacturing
Company, as previously noted, closed its Suffolk
Mills in 1936.

Losses were not confined to the group of mills
using Merrimack power. Of the mills at the upper
falls of the Concord, the Bay State Woolen Mills
(the former Faulkner mill), operated by the American Woolen Company since 1899, were closed in
1927. At the time of mapping, this plant was in
process of destruction. The Lowell Bleachery
closed its Lowell plant about 1930. The buildings
have been for the most part destroyed. The Belvidere Woolen Company, in operation since 1853,
went out of business in 1929, and the Stirling Mills,
founded in 1880, have recently ceased operations.
These mills are vacant. Of the mills at the lower

---

[1] Stone, *op. cit.*, I, 734–36.

falls on the Concord, the New England Bunting Company ceased operations in 1932. Its mill has been destroyed. The Musketaquid Mill of the United States Worsted Company was closed about 1929 and the building is now occupied by the manufacturer of paper boxes previously mentioned (p. 79).

Of the several textile companies in the railroad industrial area, the New England Southern Mills, a cotton company only recently established in the city and occupying the large factory buildings at the junction of Pawtucket Street and Broadway (Map V), discontinued manufacturing in 1929. The mills are vacant. The Ram's Head Mills near the western end of Middlesex Street, operated until recently by the American Woolen Company, were utilized for a short time by another textile company, but now the only occupant is a manufacturer of paper boxes. The Shaw Stocking Company, which was established in 1877 and built a large plant on Chelmsford Street, discontinued the manufacture of hosiery in 1931. There were other casualties among lesser textile companies.

Among nontextile companies, notable losses were the Kitson Machine Shop, which had become a subsidiary of the Saco-Lowell Shops, the C. F. Hatch Company, manufacturers of paper boxes, and the Lowell division of the United States Bobbin and Shuttle Company. The Kitson plant included two large mill buildings opposite the Saco-Lowell Shops on Dutton Street, one of which is now utilized in part by The Giant Store. The Hatch Company occupied a factory on Thorndike Street next the railroad; the United States Bobbin and Shuttle Company was one of those operating along the railway extension between the upper and the lower falls of the Concord.

These many losses were of course a staggering blow to the city. Even as the losses were in progress, however, partial recovery was under way. It has been indicated that of the eleven corporations composing the central mill ring the first to discontinue operations were the Middlesex Company and the Bigelow Carpet Company. The property of these companies was only in part occupied by the Ipswich Mills and the Columbia Textile Company, and portions of it were taken over by other establishments which have remained substantial additions to the city. By 1920, the Middlesex plant provided space for the Gilet Carbonizing Company (wool-scouring and carbonizing), the Lowell Felt Company, the Bagshaw Company (textile pins and phonograph needles), the Merrimack Utilization Company (cotton waste), and the Hy-Carbo Steel Company, all of which still occupy this site, as well as for the Ipswich Mills. After the Ipswich Mills ceased operations, the real estate (though not the Merrimack power rights) reverted in time to the original owner, the Middlesex Company, which, no longer a manufacturing corporation, administers its mills and its power rights on the Concord River for the utilization of its tenants. Additional companies were added to the group as more space became available, and today only about one-twentieth of the rentable floor space in the buildings owned by the Middlesex Company remains unoccupied. The Gilet Carbonizing Company has acquired ownership of one of the buildings of the group.

The mills of the Bigelow Carpet Company also were taken over in part by their present occupants before the exodus of the cotton mills began. In 1923, the Newmarket Manufacturing Company of Newmarket, New Hampshire, silk and rayon manufacturers, established a branch factory known as the "Lowell Silk Mills" in one of the units of the Bigelow plant, and in 1929 acquired additional space and transferred all its operations from Newmarket to this site. Also before 1925 two worsted manufacturers, the J. M. and E. M. Abbot Company, later absorbed by the Abbot Worsted Company of Graniteville, Massachusetts, and the Uxbridge Worsted Company of Uxbridge, Massachusetts, began manufacturing in another of the mills of the Bigelow plant, while still another unit was occupied by Conant, Houghton, and Company, now a branch of the United Elastic Corporation. The Newmarket and Abbot companies purchased their mills and the Abbot Company provides space for the Uxbridge Company; one mill building was sold to a storage company and one for use as a garage.

` Some buildings were destroyed. The real estate not otherwise disposed of and the total power rights of the former Lowell Corporation are the property of the Assets Realization Company, not a manufacturing concern. This company has the United Elastic Corporation and the Union Crayon Company as tenants, rents additional space to the Newmarket Company, and supplies power to both owners and tenants within the group wherever needed. It has additional space available for disposal.

The cotton mills which were vacated between 1925 and 1930 had less opportunity to become reoccupied, since large amounts of available space were thrown upon the market within a few years and the general depression in the country as a whole after 1929 discouraged new ventures in business. Much space was, however, gradually taken up by manufacturers and some by commercial concerns. The Appleton Company, now manufacturing in South Carolina, retains ownership of its mills and power rights in Lowell and supplies space and power to numerous tenants. Except for some buildings which have been destroyed and one sold for use by a storage company, the real estate and power of the former Massachusetts Mills, as well as the power rights on the Merrimack formerly owned by the Middlesex Company, are the property of the Lowell Industrial Development Company, which also supplies space and power to many tenants.

Some of the mills of the Hamilton Company have

been sold to various owners—the Lowell Ice Company (manufacturers), the Courier Citizen Company (printers and publishers [p. 43]), the Lowell Motor Sales Company and the Middlesex Supply Company (commercial concerns). One building is used for a garage. The entire bleaching and finishing plant was razed. The remaining property is controlled by Marden and Murphy, local real-estate agents, and is occupied in considerable part by the Megowen Educator Food Company (p. 43). The remainder is offered for rent. The Courier Citizen Company supplies space to the Laganas Shoe Company and the Lowell Electrotype Foundry. The water power of the Hamilton Company is leased by the Newmarket Manufacturing Company, which, owning no power in its own right, utilizes the power developed through the Hamilton wheels for its own operations.

The Lawrence Company, having discontinued hosiery manufacture, occupies less plant than formerly. It has sold one mill to the Hub Hosiery Company and one to a manufacturer of paper products. The plant also provides space for a worsted manufacturing company and a company manufacturing textile machinery, which are controlled by the same interests as the Lawrence Company. It has some additional vacant space, not, however, for the most part rentable because of inaccessibility. It supplies power to the affiliated companies.

The Merrimack Company and the Boott Mills

have not let space to other manufacturing concerns. The Merrimack Company owns the former Tremont power as well as retaining its own original power rights, but a large part of the Tremont plant has been destroyed. The status of the Suffolk Mills has been previously noted. The Suffolk power rights are owned by the Nashua Company though not at present utilized. The permanent power owned by the Saco-Lowell Shops is leased by the Appleton Company, which ordinarily uses the water through its own wheels but which at times of exceptional pressure secures somewhat more power by operating the water wheels of the former machine shop.[1]

All the water power developed by the various companies is converted into electricity, and it is therefore possible to arrange for the transmission of power from one plant to another, thus avoiding waste of power by one company while another has a shortage. The Assets Realization, Appleton, and Hamilton (Newmarket) systems are thus linked together; the Newmarket system, in turn, is connected with that of the Lowell Electric Light Corporation, so that any one of the three companies may obtain supplementary power from that source when it is needed. The Middlesex Company supplements Concord power with power purchased from the Lowell Industrial Development Com-

---

[1] These are below the surface in the vacant area where the machine shop formerly stood.

pany, which now owns the former Middlesex rights on the Merrimack.

The five companies of the central mill ring which are owners of mill property, but not themselves manufacturers, and which offer space for rental to other companies own at present approximately 2,500,000 square feet of floor space. Of this, about 700,000 square feet are vacant, while about 1,800,000 square feet are rented for manufacturing, storage, or, in a few cases, commercial enterprises. Floor space owned by the three cotton companies which are still operating is estimated at between 3,500,000 and 4,000,000 square feet. Of this, perhaps 20 per cent is at present unoccupied but not offered for rental. The Suffolk Mills represent an additional 725,000 square feet of working and storage space now idle but not vacated. Approximately 1,300,000 square feet has been sold to manufacturing companies (including the Courier Citizen Company, printers). Space sold to storage companies and other commercial concerns is estimated at not far from 500,000 square feet.

Beyond the central mill ring, the plant of the former Shaw Stocking Company on Chelmsford Street provides space for several industrial concerns. The buildings are owned separately by several manufacturing companies which offer for rental the space not utilized by their own establishments. A filling station, an oil company, and a garage occupy portions of the quadrangle. Not all of the available space is utilized. A company manufacturing furniture has moved from another location in the city into the former mill of the United States Bobbin and Shuttle Company; the former Hatch Company factory opposite South Common on Thorndike Street is partially occupied by a clothing manufacturer and a wholesale grocer. A clothing company, a knitting company, a paper tube manufacturer, and the Heinze Electric Company occupy buildings in the yard of the Wamesit Power Company, space here having been vacated by the United States Cartridge Company.

The manufacturing companies now operating in the mills vacated by the former textile corporations are in part newly organized companies, in part established companies which moved to the city from their previous places of manufacture or which maintain establishments elsewhere and opened branch factories in Lowell, in part companies which previously occupied less desirable locations within Lowell and moved into the central factory group when space there became available. They range in size from very small concerns to large ones employing on the average nearly a thousand workers. The Newmarket Manufacturing Company and the Suffolk Knitting Company, which occupies space in the Appleton plant, operate the largest two establishments. Products of very wide variety are manufactured by the many companies. Shoes, hosiery, mops, mill supplies, hair tonic, furniture polish, ice cream, paper products, and other commodities are all manufactured within the plant of a single former cotton corporation.

It is apparent that, while the location and form of the several industrial areas have been long established, the distribution of industries within the areas, especially within the central industrial area, is in large part the product of recent changes. It has been shown that thirty years ago the original mill semicircle was occupied chiefly by cotton manufacturers, varied only by one woolen company, one carpet manufacturer, and one machine shop. Even fifteen years ago this pattern was not greatly altered. Woolen and worsted manufacturing companies, established for the most part too late to share in the use of Merrimack power, were in large measure concentrated at the two falls of the Concord. Other industries, and some later established textile plants, occupied the railroad areas or were scattered elsewhere. The confused pattern of today (Map V) results largely from the movement of diverse industries into the vacated textile mills. Abundant floor space, power, water for industrial purposes if needed, transportation facilities, all are offered by these mills, and many industries make no further demands upon their sites. Tanneries, breweries, lumber mills, fertilizer works, foundries will, for obvious reasons, not be involved in the migration. The concentration of the boot and shoe industry in the portion of the central industrial area

extending from the mouth of the Concord to near
the bridge over the Pawtucket Canal at Broadway
(p. 52) means only that it is the eastern part of this
area which contains most of the vacated textile mills
and which therefore provides space for the newcomers among the shoe companies, while the western
part of the area is the region of varied manufactures
which developed adjoining the early textile ring
and was a natural choice for the older establishments of an industry which did not demand mar-
ginal location. Textile industries still predominate
in the central area partly because of the survival
of some of the early textile companies and partly
because textile companies are important among the
newcomers who occupy the vacated mills. Lowell's
labor supply skilled in textile industries and its wide
reputation in textile manufacture increase its attraction to manufacturers of this class. It is a textile
city still.

While the establishment of many smaller manufacturing companies in the mills of the former large
corporations has provided much employment, nevertheless the city's industries, as previously stated,
employed about 15,000 fewer workers in 1936 than
in 1919. This loss, combined with the movement of
workers to homes in the outer portions of the city
previously described, resulted in decreased population in the central areas, lessened demand for
residential and commercial space, devaluation of
property. But assessed valuations, based upon the

values of earlier years, tend to remain high, property is consumed by taxes and mortgages, and destruction of buildings and ownership by banks or city seem an inevitable consequence. Gradual movement of resident population from the central areas of cities has of course been the result of improved transportation everywhere. But in growing cities with expanding industry or commerce, vacated residential property near the heart of the city tends to be utilized by industrial or commercial establishments, which are increasing in numbers. In Lowell, natural decentralization of population has been, unfortunately, coincident with decrease of industry, and a serious problem has ensued.

It has been shown how the city's pattern evolved as its industries grew and what modifications were later wrought by industrial losses. It remains to consider the bases for industrial rise and decline.

CHAPTER 4

Factors in Industrial Rise
and Decline

Power

THE STORY of Lowell's origin and growth has made it apparent that in the early stages of development power was a factor of first importance. The availability of abundant and easily developed water power was the primary consideration in the choice of the site for the Merrimack Manufacturing Company and doubtless in the selection of the new settlement as the location for the textile companies which followed before 1840. It was also a significant factor in the evolution of the industrial area bordering the Concord. The function of power in the later changes in and present status of the city's industries remains to be examined.

For the lease of Merrimack water power to the early corporations, a unit of measurement was established known as a "mill-power," which was defined in the following terms: "Each mill-power or privilege at the respective Falls is declared to be the right to draw from the nearest canal or water course of the said Proprietors so much water as, during fifteen hours in every day of twenty-four hours, shall give a power equal to twenty-five cubic feet per second at the Great Fall, when the head and fall there is thirty feet. . . ."[1] "Each of the said mill-powers shall be forever subject to the yearly payment of 300 dollars for the use of said Proprietors."[2] A mill-power is the equivalent of about sixty horsepower and was sufficient to operate 3,584 spindles.[3] Cash payments were made when the leases were given and the subsequent annual payments were for the purpose of providing for the management of the power system and the maintenance of the works.[4] It is to be remembered that the manufacturers using the power became themselves the proprietors (p. 100) and that the organization known as "The Proprietors of Locks and Canals" exists for the purpose of administering the system and not for the purpose of making a profit from the sale of power.

The total number of mill-powers owned is $139 \frac{11+}{30}$. This is regarded as the permanent power, though, when mills are operating 80 hours per week, minimum flow yields sometimes as low as 50 per cent of the power owned; on a basis of 48 hours per week, 10,000 horsepower, which is slightly in excess of the mill-powers owned, represents a fair low-water average. When power in excess of the per-

---

[1] *Form of Lease of Water Power at Lowell*, p. 6.
[2] *Ibid.*, p. 10.
[3] Appleton, *op. cit.*, p. 28.
[4] *Tenth Census of the United States: 1880*, XVI, 32.

manent power is available, owners have the right to draw surplus water in amounts proportionate to the amounts of permanent power owned. The charges for surplus water are fixed from time to time by the Proprietors. Water wheels installed in the plants of the associated companies have a capacity of about 30,000 horsepower.

These arrangements make the cost of permanent power to the owners low, about two mills per kilowatt-hour. The cost of surplus power varies, but now amounts to about five mills per kilowatt-hour.

Estimates of different manufacturers vary as to the cost of generating steam power. Direct comparisons of the relative costs of water power and steam power in the same establishment are possible in few cases, since few companies utilizing both types of power remain. A representative of one of the large corporations reports that the cost of generating steam power approximates the cost of surplus water power but that he believes the water power to be slightly cheaper. A second company agrees that the water power is slightly cheaper. Another of the corporations gives a considerably higher figure for steam power. One variable in the cost of steam power is the extent to which steam is used for purposes other than power; if the same steam is used for processing, such as dyeing and bleaching, a part of the cost of generation will properly be charged against these departments and the cost assigned to power be thus reduced. The New

England Power Association reports that this double use of steam so far reduces costs that public utilities companies cannot compete in supplying electric power for large plants such as woolen and worsted factories using large amounts of steam for processing.

In the development of steam power, Lowell manufacturers are at some disadvantage as compared with those in New England seaboard cities because of the cost of transporting the fuel from tidewater. Boston and Maine freight rates from Boston to Lowell are 80½¢ per gross ton for bituminous coal in carload lots and 6¢ per 100 pounds for fuel oil in tank cars (estimated weight 7.4 pounds per gallon). A rate of 5½¢ per 100 pounds on "Bunker C" industrial fuel oil in tank cars was published in June, 1938. The rate on coal carried by Boston and Maine trucks to Lowell from Boston, Everett, or Chelsea, Massachusetts, or from Pawtucket, Providence, or Warwick, Rhode Island, is 90¢ per gross ton. Of the three cotton corporations (Lawrence Company, making knit goods but still spinning cotton, included), two burn only oil; the third uses either coal or oil depending upon varying rates. The oil used is chiefly Venezuelan oil brought to Boston or Everett by water and trucked to Lowell at rates approximating the rail rates. The coal used comes from Pocahontas or New River, West Virginia, is shipped from Virginia ports by water to Boston and thence by rail

to Lowell. The cost of producing steam power at
a large steam generating plant in Boston in 1937
was $4\frac{1}{3}$ mills per kilowatt-hour. This includes the
cost of fuel, water, and labor in the generating
plant; no delivery costs are included. This is
somewhat below the lowest of the figures quoted for
Lowell.

The plant of the Lowell Electric Light Corporation is a steam generating plant, burning Pennsylvania coal and using Concord River water for boilers and condensing. It is a member of the New
England Power Association, a holding company
whose subsidiary companies operate numerous and
widely scattered generating plants in Massachusetts, Rhode Island, New Hampshire, and Vermont. The New England Power Company, a major
subsidiary, owns a series of power plants on the
Connecticut and Deerfield Rivers and sells power
wholesale to large industrials and to public utility
companies. The purpose of the New England
Power system is to connect water power developed
chiefly on the Connecticut and Deerfield with steam
power on the Atlantic seaboard. The Narragansett
Power Company in Providence operates the largest
steam generating plant in the New England Power
group and the Boston Edison Company provides
also a large source of steam-developed power. Link-
ing hydroelectric and steam plants permits the
development of the hydroelectric plants to a capacity which would be impractical without the possi-

bility of dependence upon steam auxiliaries to regulate the supply of power. Costs of generating steam power increase with increasing distance from the coast, but costs of delivery of hydroelectric power decrease as inland sources of water power are approached. The effect of connecting the coastal stations, the inland water-power stations, and many intervening local plants is a tendency toward equalization of power rates throughout the area served. Each company is, however, a unit, and lack of uniformity of rates is introduced by local circumstances.

A high voltage transmission line extends 126 miles from Fifteen Mile Falls on the upper Connecticut River, where the largest hydroelectric plant in New England is located, to a substation in Tewksbury, a short distance east of Lowell. With this the Lowell plant is connected. The capacity of the Lowell company's plant is, however, adequate for its needs and its contract with the New England Power Company is for surplus power only. Surplus power is furnished at low rates, but customers can buy it only when there is a surplus available. Companies having contracts for surplus power only may find it advantageous to buy power when surplus power is offered at rates lower than their own generating costs.

The industrial power rates of the Lowell Electric Light Corporation now in effect (1938) are as follows: (1) a rate for small consumers rang-

ing from 8¢ per kilowatt-hour for the first 400
kilowatt-hours delivered monthly to 3¢ per kilowatt-hour for all electricity delivered each month
in excess of 1,200 kilowatt-hours; (2) a rate for
larger consumers ranging from 3.5¢ per kilowatt-hour for the first 4,700 kilowatt-hours delivered monthly to 1¢ per kilowatt-hour for all
electricity delivered each month in excess of 510,000
kilowatt-hours; (3) a complicated rate including an
investment charge based upon demand and an
electricity charge of 3.1¢ per kilowatt-hour for
power delivered; discounts are applied based upon
the demand in horsepower. Schedules (2) and (3)
carry a clause providing for an increase of charge
of 1/100 of a mill per kilowatt-hour for each 1-cent
increase in the cost of coal above $7 per gross
ton. In making any comparison of power costs to
the consumer supplied by a public utilities company
with direct generating costs, it is to be remembered
that there is always a wide spread between the two
because capital charges for plant and for delivery
equipment add greatly to the final cost. The companies developing Merrimack water power and selling it to their tenants are able to offer power at
rates somewhat lower than those of the Lowell Electric Light Corporation, since their generating costs
are low and delivery costs are reduced by the smallness of the area served by each company. Also
their power supply is somewhat less regular than
that of the public utilities company and lower rates

are offered as an inducement to manufacturers to occupy their space and use their power.

Almost all of the power used in the city is electric. The electrification of the plants using Merrimack power was completed by 1930. A summary of the sources from which the various manufacturing companies obtain power follows. The three surviving manufacturers of the original corporations generate their own power, supplementing Merrimack power when necessary with the product of their own steam generating plants. The other occupants of the old textile mill ring are, with a few exceptions, supplied with power by one or another of the other owners of Merrimack power and the Middlesex Company. These owners supply their tenants with steam for heat but do not now use steam for generating power. As has been indicated, supplementary power is sometimes furnished by the Lowell Electric Light Corporation, and a few companies occupying purchased buildings obtain all their power from this source. Manufacturers composing the group at the upper falls of the Concord are supplied in part with power by the Wamesit Power Company. One cotton waste company has a small water power on River Meadow Brook. Manufacturers elsewhere are entirely served by the Lowell Electric Light Corporation, with the exception of some half-dozen companies who still make partial or complete use of steam power.

In considering power as a factor in the location

of industry, it must be recognized that it has much less importance than formerly in influencing choice of location because of the present facilities for the wide distribution of electric power and the tendency toward equalization of rates brought about by such mergers as are illustrated by the New England Power Association. Moreover, except in such industries as the electrochemical or electrometallurgical industries, the cost of power represents only a small percentage of the total cost of manufacture —about 2 to 3 per cent in an ordinary cotton mill; and it will therefore be much less significant than such an item as labor costs, which in many industries makes up a large fraction of the total expense of manufacture, in influencing decisions as to the location of industrial plants.

However, in seeking reasons for Lowell's recent loss of a large part of its cotton industry, which is the major loss which it has suffered, the possibility that the power situation was a factor in this loss should not be overlooked. A comparison with New England's chief competitor in the cotton industry, the Southern Appalachian Piedmont, is at once suggested. A recent study of the cotton industry of this region in which detailed comparisons are made with the cotton industry of New England as to costs of manufacture comes to the conclusion that "textile mills in the Southern Appalachian Piedmont can produce their own power as cheaply as those of New England and can buy their power at a slightly lower rate than can New England factories." [1] About five to eight mills per kilowatt-hour is given as the average cost of producing steam power in factories in which the exhaust steam from the turbines is used for processing.[2] These figures correspond approximately with the estimates obtained for mills in Lowell making similar use of steam (p. 120). Lemert's conclusion that purchased power in the Piedmont is slightly cheaper than in New England is based upon a comparison of the rates of the Boston Edison Company and the Public Utilities Commission of Rhode Island with those of the Duke Power Company of North Carolina and the Georgia Power Company. The comparison has no bearing upon Lowell, since the present cotton companies do not and the former companies did not purchase power except, at times, from their associated companies. As has been shown, the cost of water power to the manufacturers in Lowell is extraordinarily low and falls well below the lowest figure given by Lemert for purchased power, which figure is based upon a high level of consumption (8.196 mills per kilowatt, with 2,000,000 kilowatt-hours used monthly: Georgia Power Company).[3] Since the majority of the textile mills in the Piedmont use purchased power, it appears that Lowell

---

[1] B. F. Lemert, *The Cotton Textile Industry of the Southern Appalachian Piedmont* (Chapel Hill: University of North Carolina Press, 1933), p. 99.

[2] *Ibid.*, p. 100.

[3] *Ibid.*, p. 103.

has not been at a disadvantage in the matter of power costs as compared with that area.

On the other hand, the relatively low power rates which the companies now developing Merrimack power have been able to offer were a factor in the decisions of some of the manufacturers now occupying the abandoned textile mills to take up locations there.

Water for Processing

To all textile manufacturers who scour or dye raw stock or who wash, full, bleach, or dye their products, the softness of the water available for industrial use is a matter of importance. Both the Merrimack and the Concord supply abundant water which is excellent in this respect. The Merrimack and its tributaries flow for the most part over crystalline rocks, and the water in consequence is exceptionally low in hardness. Three analyses of Merrimack water at the head of the Lowell canals in 1936 show a hardness of 10 parts per million on June 9, 14 on August 28, 17 on November 19.[1] Eleven analyses made at earlier periods show an average hardness of 11.2 parts per million.[2] For comparison, the Connecticut at Northfield Farms has a hardness of about 29; the Housatonic (East

---

[1] Data from records kept at the experiment station of the State Board of Health at Lawrence.

[2] U. S. G. S. Water Supply and Irrigation Paper 79 (Washington: Government Printing Office, 1903), p. 56.

Branch) at Pittsfield, 76; normal water from an upland region in the Ohio Basin, 43.6.[1] No analysis of Concord River water is available, but manufacturers using it state that it approximates Merrimack water in hardness. It is used by woolen and worsted manufacturers without treatment for hardness. Raw water from the city's wells on Pawtucket Boulevard ranges in hardness from about 25 to 29 and that from the wells near River Meadow Brook may run as high as 44 in hardness.

The amount of suspended matter or coloring matter which water contains has significance in connection with its use for dyeing. In spite of the fact that Nashua, a short distance upstream, pours its waste into the Merrimack, the water is described by several Lowell manufacturers as "as good as average" in its clearness and freedom from color. Simple filtering systems are used in some of the textile plants to strain out suspended matter. The Concord water contains some suspended vegetable matter which may be removed by filtration.

The owners of Merrimack power draw water from the canals for processing just as they draw water for power, and all the water used is covered by the charges which are paid for power. The amount used by the largest consumer of process water is the equivalent of about one-half of one mill-power. It is thus apparent that the cost of

---

[1] *Ibid.,* pp. 95, 101, 118.

process water to the Merrimack manufacturers is practically negligible. One manufacturer states that in a cotton mill with which he is familiar in the South the water purchased for processing costs from $1,700 to $1,800 per month. The charge for water supplied by the Lowell Water Works is 21¢ per 100 cubic feet. The use of 25 cubic feet of water per second (the equivalent of one mill-power) at this rate would cost $3.15 per minute or $189 per hour. It is thus evident that not only the softness but the cheapness of the water supplied by the rivers is an item of importance to manufacturers of Lowell.

It must, however, be recognized that systems for softening water now make possible the adaptation of hard water for process purposes and that the textile industries are less bound than formerly to sites where soft water is obtainable, though, of course, processes for water softening involve additional cost. The American Woolen Company reports that it is softening the relatively hard water of the Ohio River and using it successfully for wool scouring in its plant at Louisville, Kentucky. In this connection the following news item of April, 1938, is of interest:

The wool shop at the Wood Worsted Mill [the largest mill of the American Woolen Company at Lawrence; uses Merrimack water for processing], including the scouring and top making, has been very quiet for the last many weeks. The Wood Mill has been operating something like fifty per cent, but much of the worsted top has come from the Bradford Mill of the company at Louisville, Kentucky. It is so much more economical to do the sorting, scouring, combing, and top making at Louisville than to do it at Lawrence, that two or three carloads per week of worsted top has been coming from Louisville to Lawrence.[1]

It is thus apparent that the cost of softening water in locations where there is only hard water may be more than offset by savings in other items in the total cost of manufacture.

Raw Materials

The chief raw materials used in Lowell industries are not produced near at hand. Cotton comes principally from the Mississippi Valley and from the southwestern portion of the cotton belt; Arkansas, Mississippi, Louisiana, Alabama, and Texas are the chief sources. Some comes to Lowell by an all-rail route, but the greater part of it is sent by boat from Gulf ports to Boston or New Bedford and thence by rail or by truck to Lowell. Transportation is prepaid and included in the brokerage charges. The all-rail rates range from about 75¢ to $1.20 per hundredweight, depending upon point of origin. At present the rate on carload lots is 77¢ from Little Rock, Arkansas; 88¢ from Shreveport, Louisiana; 86¢ from Hattiesburg, Mississippi. Practically all Texas cotton moves from Galveston or Houston by water. In general, the Boston basis

---

[1] *American Wool and Cotton Reporter*, XLII (April 7, 1938), 58.

of all-rail rates on cotton from Mississippi Valley shipping points applies to all destinations in New England as far east as Lewiston, Maine. Water rates amount to about 40¢ per hundredweight from Gulf ports to Boston; the rail rate from Boston to Lowell on cotton in compressed bales is 15¢ per 100 pounds or 10½¢ from docks and fumigation plants at Boston which have direct track connection with the Boston and Maine. Cotton is trucked to Lowell from Boston by Boston and Maine trucks for 12¢ per 100 pounds if in compressed bales; the corresponding rate for cotton in uncompressed bales is 24¢ to 26¢.

Distance from source of supply would seem theoretically to put Lowell's cotton manufacturers at a disadvantage as compared with those in or near the cotton belt, while, except in the case of cotton received at the several places by all-rail routes, distance from the coast would make cotton costs in Lowell slightly higher than in Fall River or New Bedford, to which water transport is possible. Actually, proximity to the cotton belt does not constitute as much of an advantage as might be expected to Piedmont manufacturers. At present, Piedmont cotton mills are depending for much of the cotton used upon states in the central and southwestern portions of the cotton belt because of the failure of the southeastern states to produce sufficient cotton of long enough staple. Surveys in 1931 showed that 70 per cent of the cotton used in North Caro-

lina mills came from outside the state.[1] The use of
longer staple cotton by the southern mills has increased as they have increasingly manufactured
finer grades of yarn than were their product in
the earlier days of the Piedmont industry.

In 1927, which is within the five-year period during which Lowell lost most of its cotton mills, the
rail rate on cotton from Texarkana, Texas, to
Greensboro, North Carolina, was only 19½¢ per
hundredweight cheaper than the rate from the same
source to Fall River (Greensboro, $1.20; Fall
River, $1.39½).[2] All-rail rates to Lowell have
long been identical with those to Fall River. In
the case of cotton originating at Jonesboro, Arkansas, or at Oklahoma City, the differential in
favor of Greensboro was only 14¢; on cotton pro-
ceeding from more eastern points the advantage of
Greensboro was greater; 24¢ on cotton from Pick-
ens, Mississippi; on that from Opelika, Alabama,
35½¢; from Marietta, Georgia, 38¢; from New
Bern, North Carolina, 38¢; from Sumter, South
Carolina, 57¢. In the last instance the rate to New
England was almost twice the rate to Greensboro
($1.21 vs. 64¢).[3] Little cotton comes to Lowell,
however, from the more eastern sources. From
some points combined rail and water rates to Lowell
are lower than the all-rail rates and the differentials
are thus reduced. On the other hand, some of the

---

[1] Lemert, *op. cit.*, p. 94.   [2] *Ibid.*, p. 97.   [3] *Ibid.*

cotton used by the Piedmont mills comes from
sources close at hand and the average cost of transportation to the southern mills is thus reduced.

The average price of cotton on the New York
market in 1927 was 20.4¢ per pound. A saving of
20¢ per hundredweight in the cost of cotton would
thus mean a saving of about 1 per cent, and a saving
of 40¢ per hundredweight a saving of about 2 per
cent in cotton costs. Assuming cost of raw material to constitute 40 per cent of total cost of manufacture,[1] a saving of 20¢ per hundredweight in cost
of cotton would mean a saving of four-tenths of
1 per cent in the cost of manufacture.

However, any conclusions as to the relative costs
of cotton to manufacturers in different localities
based directly upon data as to freight rates are liable
to serious error, because the advantages of rate
differentials do not necessarily accrue to the manufacturer. Copeland wrote in 1912, "In North
Carolina about one-fourth of the cotton used in
the mills is brought from other states, particularly
Mississippi, and the price of all the cotton is determined by the Mississippi price plus the freight
charge from Mississippi to Charlotte or to what-

---

[1] Averages of figures from 206 companies combining spinning and
weaving of cotton goods in 1933 and 1934 show raw materials constituting the following percentages of the total cost of manufacture: 46.2
per cent, January–June, 1933; 38.08 per cent, July–December, 1933;
41.11 per cent, January–June, 1934; 41.50 per cent, July–August, 1934.
Report of the Federal Trade Commission on the Textile Industries,
Part II, *The Cotton Textile Industry* (Washington: Government Printing Office, 1935), p. 17.

ever city or town it may be delivered. And the
freight rate from Mississippi to Charlotte, for
example, is nearly as high as the rate from southern
shipping points to New England." [1] The transportation charge is not paid by the manufacturer
but is prepaid and included in the broker's charge.
This gives an opportunity for some elimination of
differentials; manufacturers at varying distances
from the place where the cotton originates may
pay the same price for the cotton delivered and the
greater spread between delivered cost and cost of
delivery in the case of the nearer mills will thus be
absorbed by the brokers.

As far as evidence is available, the manufacturers themselves are of the opinion that in the
obtaining of raw materials location in the South is
of little or no advantage. Lemert draws the conclusion that the Piedmont mills do have an advantage over the New England mills in rates on cotton
"in spite of statements by Piedmont mill operators
that New England mills get their cotton as cheaply,
or cheaper, than Piedmont mills." [2] The representatives of present or former Lowell cotton companies consulted regard the raw material factor as
an insignificant one in the South's advantage.
Three of the companies represented have had experience in the operation of mills both in Lowell

---

[1] M. T. Copeland, *The Cotton Manufacturing Industry of the United States* (Cambridge: Harvard University Press, 1912), p. 36.
[2] Lemert, *op. cit.*, pp. 95–96.

and in the South. One states that the cost of cotton
in this company's own southern mill is certainly not
as much as 10¢ per hundredweight less than the
cost in its New England mill. Another reports that
though its Alabama mill depends upon cotton from
the immediate vicinity this is not considered a significant factor. The third states that the position of
the southern mills in relation to sources of raw
material constitutes almost no advantage. The inland location of Lowell as a factor in obtaining raw
materials in competition with seaboard cities in
New England is similarly regarded as negligible.

Lowell is also remote from the chief primary
sources of raw wool but it is near Boston, the chief
wool market of the country. Some wool is shipped
directly from western states to Lowell, but much
of it is bought in the Boston market. Domestic
wool from various western states is used almost
exclusively at present, though some South American wool is consumed in the manufacture of upholstery yarns. Mohair, used by the Massachusetts
Mohair Plush Company, and by the Abbot Worsted Company in the manufacture of upholstery
yarns, comes principally from Texas. Cattle hair
used together with wool in the manufacture of felt
is bought in New Jersey but comes originally from
tanneries throughout the country. Rail rates from
Boston are 23¢ per 100 pounds on scoured wool,
17¢ on wool in grease. Trucking rates on wool are
the same for twenty-seven motor carriers and are

22¢ per 100 pounds on scoured wool, 16¢ on wool tops, and 14¢ on wool in grease.

Acetate rayon yarns are obtained from Maryland and Pennsylvania, viscose rayons from Pennsylvania, Virginia, and Tennessee. Worsted yarns for use in the knit-goods industry come from New England spinners, chiefly in Massachusetts, Rhode Island, and Maine. The cotton hosiery yarns manufactured by the Lawrence Company are bought locally by hosiery manufacturers; cotton yarns used by makers of cotton small wares come in considerable part from southern spinners rather than from New England sources. Even cotton waste processed by Lowell companies is sent in part from the South.

For leather, as for wool, Boston is a principal market, though primary sources are for the most part remote. Much kid, originating in China or India, is used in the manufacture of the cheaper grades of women's shoes, which is an important branch of the industry in Lowell. There appears to be little relation between the importance of the shoe industry in Lowell and the existence there of a large plant manufacturing upper leathers. This plant tans calfskins and makes for the most part high-grade leathers.

Similarly there is, so far as materials are concerned, little relation between the development of the clothing industry or the upholstery business in Lowell and its importance as a textile center. One clothing manufacturer reports the use of the Lawrence Company's jerseys and thread of local origin, but fabrics are obtained from a great variety of sources and there is little evidence of the interdependence of these industries.

Paper and paper board used in the manufacture of paper tubes and boxes comes from Pennsylvania, South Carolina, North Carolina, and New Jersey as well as from Maine and other New England sources. Some strawboard from Holland is used. A manufacturer states that Pennsylvania producers can pay the transportation charges and still in some cases undersell New England sources.

A company manufacturing machinery gives as the sources from which the chief materials used are assembled: lumber from Lousiana and Vermont; steel from Pennsylvania and Ohio: bearings from Conecticut and New Jersey; chains and sprockets from Indiana; motors from Massachusetts and California; cast iron from Lowell. The boilerworks obtains both iron and coal from Pennsylvania. The gas company uses a high-volatile Virginia coal. Stone for the marble and granite workers comes from Barre, Vermont; Westerly, Rhode Island; Quincy, Massachusetts; Finland; and Sweden.

Markets

Markets also are widespread. The primary cotton-goods market is New York City. Much of Lowell's product is sold through New York agencies, but the consumption is nation-wide. One company reports a considerable market just now on the Pacific Coast. The fact that there is overnight transportation to New York from Lowell is held by some textile companies as a significant advantage, though others consider the importance of this factor somewhat overrated. It is clear that with the uncertain economic conditions of recent years there has been less manufacturing on order and more spot business, and ability to deliver rapidly has been of greater importance than formerly.

In so far as Piedmont manufacturers ship their manufactured products to New York, they are at a disadvantage both as to time and cost of delivery as compared with Massachusetts manufacturers. From Charlotte, North Carolina, to New York, for example, all-rail rates on cotton goods run about 50 per cent, and combined rail and water rates more than 90 per cent, higher than the corresponding rates from Lowell.[1] As southern mills have come to produce the more highly elaborated and finer qualities of goods, they have been forced to turn increasingly to the national market in order to dispose of their product.[2]

Lowell worsted manufacturers report their chief customers in eastern and middle western states. New York City is again a primary market; other cities in New York State, Cleveland, and Chicago

---

[1] *Ibid.,* p. 114.   [2] *Ibid.,* p. 149.

are good consumers. A company manufacturing mohair yarns finds its chief market for these yarns in Philadelphia, where there are plush manufacturers; it sells also to plush manufacturers in South Carolina and in Utica. The mohair plush produced in Lowell has a nation-wide market.

New York is the chief market for rayons. The Lowell rayon manufacturers produce gray goods only, and dyeing and finishing are required. This is done in part in New England, in part in the New York-New Jersey area around Union City, Passaic, or Hoboken.

Some knitted fabrics are sold to the rubber-goods trade centering in the Boston metropolitan area. Underwear, hosiery, and knitted outerwear are marketed through New York agencies, through widespread wholesale channels, or through direct retail outlets. Felt manufacturers sell their product throughout the country; one company reports also a Canadian market. Manufacturers of shoe bindings and shoelaces sell largely to the New England shoe trade and find Lowell's central position in relation to this market advantageous. Central position in relation to the New England market is also an asset to the company manufacturing industrial tapes and webbings, though it has other markets widely distributed in the United States and abroad. Covered elastic thread is sold to New England and the South. Insulated wire manufacturers serve nation-wide demand; one indicates New

York, Chicago, and the West Coast as the principal markets. Twine is sold to jobbers and five-and-ten-cent stores throughout the country. The dye works does about 70 per cent of its work for manufacturers in Lowell, and, beyond Lowell, serves other companies within a radius of about one hundred miles. The wool-scouring and carbonizing plant derives its chief business from Boston, whose wool merchants send wool to be processed before sale to manufacturers; some work, however, comes from as far west as Michigan.

Clothing manufacturers are not dependent upon near-by markets; one company reports that its principal sales are in the Middle West, the South, and the West Coast; one that it has markets on the West Coast, in Chicago, and well distributed east of Chicago; a third that some of its products are internationally known. Hats and caps are marketed in New England.

Several shoe companies indicate the entire country as their market; one specifies the northern states, one the Middle West; one explains that the market is principally east of the Mississippi, as it costs from ten to fifteen cents to deliver a pair of shoes to the Pacific Coast.

Of the paper products manufacturers, one making boxes reports the market limited to a radius of fifty miles; one making cores, tubes, and round boxes has a wide market in New England and others beyond, the farthest distant being in Texas;

this company operates a plant in Trenton to serve the New York area; a third company, making tubes, cones, and cores, gives the entire Atlantic seaboard as the area served. In each case Lowell itself provides some part, but in no case a large part, of the market.

The manufacture of foundry and machine-shop products naturally suggests itself as one to which the local market provided by an industrial city would be a significant attraction. Certainly the Lowell Machine Shop, which was in large part responsible for the city's important place in machinery manufacture, was established to equip the textile mills, and doubtless market was an important factor in the location in Lowell of other establishments for the making of machinery in the days of expanding industry. But whatever may have been the case in the past, most present manufacturers of machinery and machine parts depend little upon Lowell as a market. Most of the estimates given by them as to the portion of their product consumed by Lowell are below 5 per cent; one company gives a figure of 20 per cent, and one a figure of 50 per cent, including repair work. Neither of these companies manufactures textile machinery. Even machine repair work is not all of local origin, though some establishments serve only local demand. The Saco-Lowell Shops reported in 1920 that only one-tenth of 1 per cent of their product supplied a Lowell market. For some manufacturers of the foundry and machine-shop group, the market is restricted to New England. Others have the South or the South and the Middle Atlantic states as markets, while some report sales in other parts of the United States and in foreign countries.

To the printing, brewing, bottling, baking, and confectionery trades, the local market naturally is significant. For most establishments in these groups, Lowell and surrounding towns provide the greater part of the market, and none of those reporting has markets outside New England with the exception of the large bakery previously described, which sells to the whole eastern seaboard.

Workers in marble and granite serve a market which is in large part, but not exclusively, local. Of the remaining miscellaneous industries, some distribute their products widely, while others are dependent upon local sales.

The area which is commercially tributary to Lowell as a shopping center is restricted on the north and east by the proximity of Nashua and Lawrence. To the west and south it is of greater extent, reaching to Pepperell, Groton, Ayer, and Littleton (Map I). The external tributary area together with Lowell itself has a population of about 190,000 people,[1] who constitute a potential market for the products of local industry.

---

[1] E. F. Gerish, *Commercial Structure of New England,* United States Department of Commerce, Domestic Commerce Series No. 26 (Washington: Government Printing Office, 1929), p. 24.

Transportation

Lowell's dependence upon many areas, both near
and distant, for markets and for raw materials em-
phasizes the importance of its facilities for transportation. It has been seen that for more than a
decade of the history of the manufacturing settlement transportation was handled by horse-drawn
vehicles supplemented by the slow-toiling traffic of
the old Middlesex Canal. In 1834 "Lowell Baggage
Waggons" were advertised to leave Lowell every
Monday and Thursday, arriving in Boston every
Tuesday and Friday, and returning to Lowell each
Wednesday and Saturday.[1] Passengers were transported by stage, Boston stages leaving Lowell in
the mornings at seven, eight, and eight-thirty, and
in the afternoons at one o'clock.[2] Three or three and
a half hours were required for the journey; return
stages reached Lowell at 5 P.M. and 6 P.M.[3] A
former resident states that "in passing to and from
Boston by private conveyance between 1830 and
1835, you would hardly go one mile without meeting
a team of four or six horses, loaded with freight,
or a six-horse stage loaded with passengers."[4]
About one hundred fifty horses are said to have
been in use by those who made teaming a special

---

[1] Floyd, *op. cit.*, p. 154.
[2] *Ibid.*, pp. 151–52.
[3] *Ibid.*
[4] J. B. French, "Early Recollections of an Old Resident," *Old Residents Historical Association, Contributions,* I, 257.

business at the time of the completion of the first railroad in 1835. The price for transporting freight by this means was from $2.50 to $4.00 per ton.[1]

Besides the Boston stages, there are listed in the 1834 directory daily stages from Lowell to Worcester, Fitchburg, Groton, and Haverhill; Dover, New Hampshire, via Newburyport; Nashua and Concord, New Hampshire; Burlington, Vermont; and Albany, via Brattleboro, Vermont. On alternate days stages departed for Salem, Springfield, Lancaster, Hopkinton, and Hanover, New Hampshire.[2]

A packet boat for the accommodation of passengers was installed on the Middlesex Canal soon after its completion and ran from Middlesex Village to Charlestown; it was propelled by horse power at the rate of about four miles per hour; the fare was 50¢ for the whole distance.[3] Other boats were run both by the proprietors of the canal and by private parties. Luggage boats were required to make two and a half miles per hour.[4] Goods conveyed to and from Lowell by way of the canal in 1835 paid tonnage dues of $11,975.51.[5] When the proposal for the Boston and Lowell Railroad was being considered, the proprietors of the canal protested to the Legislature that "if the usual time

---

[1] *Ibid.*
[2] Floyd, *op. cit.,* pp. 152–54.
[3] French, "Early Recollections of an Old Resident," *op. cit.,* p. 252.
[4] Dame, *op. cit.,* p. 283.
[5] *Ibid.,* p. 285.

consumed in passing from one place to another be three hours, there seems not to be any such exigency to make that space of time half what it now is as to justify the establishment of a railroad for that purpose merely . . ." [1]

In spite of this remonstrance, the railroad was built, and it has been seen that other roads which followed in time made Lowell the focus of several radiating lines. The city's position near the great bend of the Merrimack made it a natural point of junction for the railroad extending along the north-south portion of the Merrimack Valley and thence southeastward to Boston with roads from cities in the lower portion of the valley and from other points to the southeast, south and southwest. Lowell is on the direct line of the Boston and Maine from Boston to Montreal, which follows the Merrimack Valley from Lowell to beyond Concord, New Hampshire. It is also on the direct route from Boston to many points in New Hampshire and Vermont which are reached by lines extending westward or northwestward from Nashua, Manchester, or Concord.

The Stony Brook branch of the Boston and Maine, which connects with the Nashua line at North Chelmsford just beyond the limits of Lowell, gives the city through communication via Ayer and

---

[1] *Historical Sketch of the Middlesex Canal with Remarks for the Consideration of the Proprietors,* by the Agent of the Corporation, 1843, pp. 28–29, quoted in Kengott, *op. cit.,* pp. 21–22.

Worcester with New York City. This road and also that of the New York, New Haven, and Hartford to Framingham connect with the main line of the Boston and Albany passing through Framingham and Worcester; this is continued west of Albany by the lines of the New York Central, providing through routes to Chicago. By the railroad to Andover, Lowell is connected with the main line of the Boston and Maine from Boston to Portland, which is continued by the Maine Central to Rockland, Bangor, and St. John.

Lowell is almost on the margin between the three more densely settled New England states and the three more sparsely settled ones. To the north lies the larger fraction of New England areally, but to the south the larger portion of its population. For easy communication with both sections, Lowell's position is a favorable one. In relation to the more densely settled portion of New England, however, its position is less favorable than that of Worcester, which, farther to the west and south, is centrally placed for communication with Massachusetts, Connecticut, Rhode Island, and southern New Hampshire and Vermont. Worcester has also the advantage of location on the main railroad line from Boston to Chicago. Lowell's closer proximity to Boston gives it a slight advantage in the time required for reaching terminals for coastwise shipping.

In rail communication with the Middle West and

Far West, the three southern New England states and parts of the northern states are on the same rate basis. All points pay the Boston rates, and position within the area is thus of no consequence.[1] The system of rail rates applying to interchange between New England and the area west of it but east of a line through Buffalo, Wheeling, and Pittsburgh is very complex. Rates are based roughly upon distance of haul.[2]

In communication with the South and with the Pacific Coast, water transport plays an important part. The Merchants and Miners Transportation Company, the Clyde Line, the Ocean Steamboat Company, and the Eastern Steamship Line operate between Boston and other Atlantic or Gulf ports. The Panama Canal brings the whole Pacific coastal region into a position in which "transportation rates for New England are materially less than the all-rail continental rates from points well in the interior."[3] For participation in coastwise trade, the fact that Lowell is near enough Boston to be quickly and cheaply reached by motor transport constitutes a factor of significance.

As the transmission of hydroelectric power has freed manufacturers from locations at the power sites, so the rapid development of trucking in recent

---

[1] C. E. Artman, *Industrial Structure of New England*, U. S. Department of Commerce, Domestic Commerce Series No. 28 (Washington: Government Printing Office, 1930), p. 95.

[2] *Ibid.*, p. 96.

[3] *Ibid.*, p. 100.

years has freed them in part from dependence upon railroads. Each of the present and former cotton mills of Lowell has its own railway siding; yet a cotton manufacturer reports that 99 per cent of the finished products of his mill leave the plant by truck. Trucks are operated in part by the railroad companies but also by many private concerns.

The trucks of the Boston and Maine Transportation Company serve Lowell on the following schedule. One truck picks up freight in Lowell early in the morning, arriving in Boston about 9:30 A.M., and returns to Lowell at about 2 P.M. Between noon and 4 P.M. approximately eight trucks leave Lowell. These load at the various mills and arrive in Boston in time to make connection with boats of the Eastern, Merchants and Miners, and other steamship lines. They also deliver to carloading companies such as the National, Universal, and Acme Fast Freight, which receive freight until 5:30 P.M. Goods carried by the steamship companies are delivered the following morning in New York City and the second morning in ports farther south on the Atlantic Coast. The carloading companies give a fast service for cotton piece goods, blankets, and other textile commodities to all parts of the country. The afternoon trucks from Lowell load freight at the terminals and elsewhere in Boston late in the afternoon and return to Lowell between eight and nine o'clock, the freight being delivered early the following morning. A last truck leaves Lowell at about 10 P.M., bringing in any late freight which has accumulated at the Lowell terminal and receiving in Boston freight for Lowell which has come in on late trucks from Portland, Dover, Keene, Fitchburg, and Springfield. This truck returns to Lowell at about 2 A.M., delivering the freight in the morning.

While many companies make use of this combined truck and boat service to New York, some prefer to ship products the whole distance to New York, or even to Philadelphia, by truck, obtaining thus even more rapid service. One trucking concern operates a regular service to New York, trucks leaving Lowell on the hour from nine to one every night and delivering in New York the following morning. Another company transports twice weekly to Philadelphia, leaving Lowell at night and delivering in Philadelphia at about noon the following day. One of the cotton corporations, one of the worsted companies, and one of the chief clothing manufacturers are included among those which ship to New York entirely by truck. The all-truck rates to New York differ little from those for combined truck and boat transport.

For manufacturers having important markets in New England, much transportation is by truck. A paper-tube company reports that trucks are used, in general, for delivery within a radius of one hundred fifty miles. Beyond that, rail transportation is employed. Such companies may own their own trucks or may hire trucking companies to deliver.

In summary, it may be said that trucks are used in very large part for delivery to near-by points; that the greater part of the transportation to New York and Philadelphia is by combined truck and boat or entirely by truck; that combined truck and boat, or truck, boat, and rail, is very generally used for shipment to the South; that principally rail transport is used for shipment to the interior. In the transportation of raw materials, rail shipments seem to retain a more important place than in the delivery of finished products, though, as has been seen, much oil, wool, and some cotton move into Lowell by truck.

For the transportation of passengers, Lowell is served both by railroads and motorbusses. The Boston and Maine operates some eighteen trains and eight busses each way daily between Boston and Lowell. All the busses from Boston continue to Manchester and most of them to Concord. More than half the trains originate or stop in Lowell. The train time to Boston ranges from thirty minutes to an hour; the bus time is about an hour. There are four daily trains through Lowell to Montreal. Frequent service to Worcester is maintained by a combination of Boston and Maine trains and busses, some of which give through transportation to New York. Blueway Trailways operate busses through Lowell between New York and

Haverhill. The Vermont Transit Company and Frontier Coach Lines offer bus service to Burlington and Montreal. Within Lowell and between Lowell and its suburbs, transportation is provided by the busses of the Eastern Massachusetts Street Railway Company, which handles intra-urban service in various New England cities.

Labor

From their beginning, Lowell's textile industries have attracted an abundant supply of labor, first from the meager farms of New England, and later from foreign sources. The recent decrease of employment has left a surplus of experienced textile labor, which has without question been a major factor in the location of new textile companies in Lowell following the removal of the large corporations. Almost every textile company replying to a question as to the advantages which Lowell offers as a place for its operations notes the abundance of experienced labor as an important factor. When there are many from whom to choose, it is possible to select the best. Spinners and weavers, as a natural consequence of Lowell's history, are more numerous than those skilled in knitting, and one company reports some difficulty in securing enough experienced knitters.

The workers trained in the textile trades but not now employed in them, together with labor experienced in other types of manufacture, and untrained labor constitute a large body of potential workers upon which the nontextile industries may draw. Shifts from one industry to another, however, are often difficult. Some companies manufacturing clothing or knitted outerwear report a shortage of experienced cutters and stitchers, and well-trained workers for the shoe industry are not always available in sufficient numbers. Many manufacturers, however, in various nontextile industries state that abundance of labor, or abundance of skilled labor, is one of the advantages which Lowell offers to them.

Lowell has for the most part had a reputation for relatively little labor trouble. Recent difficulties in the shoe industry have to some extent dissipated this reputation. The textile industries in Lowell are not highly organized. It is said that the French do not unionize readily and are much less susceptible to labor agitation than, for example, the Italians who constitute a large element in the population of Lawrence. Only from some shoe manufacturers does there come the complaint of "troublesome" or "unreasonable" labor. One employer states that Lowell's workers "desire principally the chance to work."

The question of labor costs is one of great importance in connection with any discussion of the bases for the areal distribution of industry. For 206 companies operating cotton mills combining spinning and weaving, average cost of labor in the

four semesters of 1933 and 1934 constituted from
27.62 to 28.59 per cent of the total cost of manufacture.[1] For 79 woolen and worsted companies
combining spinning and weaving, cost of labor in
the same periods made up between 31 and 34 per
cent of the total cost of manufacture.[2] In almost
all industries cost of labor is an important element
in total cost.

In the cotton industry for the country as a whole,
as compared with many other industries, wages have
been relatively low; a compilation made up by
the National Industrial Conference Board from
the United States Census of Manufactures (1914)
showed that the average annual earnings of workers in cotton mills were 33 per cent less than the
average for workers in twenty-three leading industries.[3] This is partly because of the very high degree
of mechanization in the cotton industry. "Not only
is the work highly automatic, but much of it is very
light." [4] It is also because any average for the cotton
industry for the country as a whole reflects the relatively low wages paid to southern labor. Conclusions
based upon such an average will not necessarily ap-
ply to New England. For example, average individ-

---

[1] *Report of the Federal Trade Commission on the Textile Industries,*
Part II, p. 17.

[2] *Ibid.,* Part III, p. 10.

[3] National Industrial Conference Board, *Hours of Work as Related
to Output and Health of Workers, Cotton Manufacturing,* Research
Report No. 4, March, 1918, p. 4.

[4] *Ibid.,* p. 3.

ual hourly earnings in the cotton industry in the United States in 1924 amounted to 37.2¢ per hour, but for Massachusetts alone, earnings in this industry were 47.3¢ per hour.[1] In the woolen and worsted industry, average hourly earnings for the country, excluding ᵥsouthern mills, in 1924 were 53.3¢ per hour,[2] and in the boot and shoe industry for the whole country 51.6¢ per hour.[3] Comparable figures for these two industries in Massachusetts are not available for 1924; in 1932 hourly earnings in both industries in Massachusetts were somewhat higher than in the country as a whole.[4] Thus wages in the cotton industry even in Massachusetts have apparently been lower than those in the other two of the state's three major industries.[5] This conclusion is further supported by the data presented in Table 2.

It is said by some that, because of this tendency toward relatively low wages in the cotton industry, other industries are at some advantage in a town in which the major industry is cotton manufacture,

---

[1] Calculated from figures in U. S. Bureau of Labor Statistics, *Wages and Hours of Labor in Cotton Goods Manufacturing, 1924,* Bulletin No. 371 (Washington: Government Printing Office, 1925), p. 11.

[2] U. S. Bureau of Labor Statistics, *Wages and Hours of Labor in Woolen and Worsted Goods Manufacturing, 1932,* Bulletin No. 584 (Washington: Government Printing Office, 1933), p. 2.

[3] U. S. Bureau of Labor Statistics, *Wages and Hours of Labor in the Boot and Shoe Industry, 1910–1932,* Bulletin No. 579 (Washington: Government Printing Office, 1933), p. 3.

[4] U. S. Bureau of Labor Statistics, Bulletin No. 584, p. 42; Bulletin No. 579, p. 22.

[5] In 1936 cotton goods failed for the first time to be among the first three industries.

TABLE 2

Workers in the Three Leading Industries of Massachusetts Classified on the Basis of Weekly Wages in the Week of Employment of Greatest Number, 1921*

Industry	Percentages of Total Numbers of Workers Receiving		
	Less Than $16	$16 or More but Less Than $25	$25 or More
Cotton goods..............	27	55	18
Woolen and worsted goods..	20	50	30
Boots and shoes...........	18	32	50

*Percentages calculated from data in Commonwealth of Massachusetts, *Statistics of Manufactures, 1921*, pp. 44, 51, 78.

because they can attract labor by offering somewhat higher wages than are paid in the cotton mills, but which are at the same time slightly lower than the wage levels for the same occupations in other cities. It has proved impossible to check such statements because insufficient data for separate cities are available, and generalizations based upon a few instances are dangerous. It seems to be true that, whatever the case may be in the initiation of a new industry in a cotton town, after establishments engaging in that industry multiply and the industry becomes well established, wage scales tend to become adjusted to those for the same industry in neighboring cities, and any advantage which may have existed originally is lost. For example, present wages in the worsted industry in Lowell approximate those in effect in Lawrence, in which worsted manufacture has long been the major industry. It is possible, however, that the wage situation in cotton may have been a factor in the development of certain other industries in Lowell and that it may have helped to promote diversity of industry, which is certainly greater in Lowell than is the case in Lawrence.

In the competition of the southern cotton industry with New England industry, the cost of labor has been a factor of major importance. Table 3 shows the average wages and the hours of work which were in effect in the cotton mills of the chief cotton manufacturing states in 1924, just preceding the departure of the first of the cotton corporations from Lowell.

It is apparent not only that the average hourly wage in Massachusetts was nearly double that in Alabama, and almost 50 per cent higher than that in North Carolina, but that Massachusetts mills were operating upon approximately a forty-eight-hour week; not only in southern states, but also in other New England states, longer working periods were everywhere in force. A decrease in the number of working hours does not, of course, affect the cost of labor per unit of product if the hourly wage and hourly product remain the same. Unless, how-

TABLE 3

Average Earnings and Hours in the Cotton-Goods Industry in 1924*

State	One-Week Pay Period†			Two-Week Pay Period†		
	Average Earnings per Hour	Average Full-Time Hours per Pay Period	Average Full-Time Earnings per Pay Period	Average Earnings per Hour	Average Full-Time Hours per Pay Period	Average Full-Time Earnings per Pay Period
Massachusetts..	$0.459	48.4	$22.22	$0.511	96.2	$49.16
Maine.........	.379	54.3	20.58	.496	97.1	53.62
New Hampshire	.458	54.0	24.73	.507	108.1	54.81
Rhode Island...	.431	51.5	22.20	.530	103.3	54.75
Connecticut....	.434	51.5	22.35	.496	101.1	50.15
New York.....	.450	49.6	22.32	.541	100.0	54.10
Alabama.......	.235	54.8	12.88	.254	114.4	29.06
Georgia........	.252	56.3	14.19	.303	112.1	33.97
North Carolina.	.311	55.5	17.26	.346	110.6	38.27
South Carolina.	.253	55.1	13.94	.317	110.0	34.87

* A total of 114 establishments included in the survey. U. S. Bureau of Labor Statistics, Bulletin No. 371, p. 11.

† Hourly wages shown for the two-week pay period are higher than for the one-week pay period because all weavers were included in the two-week group and weaving is a relatively highly paid occupation.

ever, productivity per hour is correspondingly increased, reduction of hours does increase production costs, since the overhead represented by machinery and plant must be charged against a smaller product. Investigations of the National Industrial Conference Board in 1918 led to the conclusion that the reduction in hours per week in northern cotton mills from fifty-eight or fifty-six to fifty-five or fifty-four did not, in general, appreciably increase the efficiency of operations and did therefore lead to an almost proportional reduction of output.[1] The forty-eight-hour week first became effective in Massachusetts in 1920 as the result of legislation restricting to forty-eight the number of working hours for women in industrial employment. A fifty-four-hour week had been previously permitted.

Massachusetts cotton manufacturers state that not only the limitation in number of working hours but other legislative regulations applying to labor have been factors in increasing manufacturing costs in Massachusetts. One illustration is the "six o'clock law" the suspension of which in 1936 was reported to have "definitely stopped the textile migration from Massachusetts."[2] The suspension permitted women, under certain regulations, to work in the textile industry until 10 P.M., thus making possible the operation of two shifts and giving Massachusetts a better opportunity for competition with other states. Regulations governing the maintenance of firemen and elevator operators, and other similar provisions are cited as further examples of legislation which contributes to the mounting of labor costs.

---

[1] National Industrial Conference Board, *op. cit.,* p. 57.

[2] *Boston Herald,* March 7, 1937.

It has proved impossible to obtain adequate data for comparing wage rates in Lowell with those in other cities and towns in Massachusetts. Such facts as are available seem to indicate that Lowell rates are at least as high as the average for the state.

Since 1924 the wage differential between Massachusetts and the South has decreased, though it remains a significant factor. Table 4 shows the aver-

TABLE 4

Average Earnings and Hours in Cotton Manufacture in September, 1937*

Region	Male Workers			Female Workers		
	Average Hourly Earnings	Average Hours Worked per Week	Average Weekly Earnings	Average Hourly Earnings	Average Hours Worked per Week	Average Weekly Earnings
United States..	$0.458	37.3	$17.08	$0.418	34.9	$14.60
Massachusetts..	.521	38.6	20.09	.466	35.4	16.51
Other New England states...	.525	38.5	20.20	.462	36.0	16.66
Middle Atlantic states.......	.592	39.5	23.37	.461	33.9	15.66
Alabama.......	.389	38.7	15.03	.375	37.4	14.03
Georgia........	.430	35.3	15.18	.368	32.9	12.09
North Carolina.	.444	36.9	16.41	.413	33.8	13.94
South Carolina.	.422	35.3	14.91	.373	33.1	12.37

* A total of 133 establishments included in the survey. M. A. Beney, *Differentials in Industrial Wages and Hours in the United States*, National Industrial Conference Board Studies, No. 239 (New York: National Industrial Conference Board, 1938), pp. 44, 54.

age wages prevailing in the cotton industry in September, 1937, and the average number of hours actually worked per week. (Figures for hours are not comparable with those in Table 3 which represent full-time working hours.) A reduction of full-time working hours to forty in all states was brought about in 1934 by the adoption of a "code of fair competition" under the National Recovery Administration. Observance of this code later ceased to be obligatory, but the majority of textile manufacturers are said to have voluntarily abided by it in respect to hours. The forty-hour week is general in the textile industries of Lowell.

The changing status of the differential between northern and southern wages in the cotton industry in the years from 1890 to the present is illustrated by the data in Table 5, in which wages for spinners and weavers in Massachusetts are compared with wages for workers in the same occupations in South Carolina. The data show that from 1890 until 1920, in spite of some reverses, the general trend was a gradual decrease in the differential. In 1890 the hourly wages for spinners and weavers in South Carolina were 33 per cent and 52 per cent, respectively, of the corresponding rates in Massachusetts. In 1920 the South Carolina rates constituted 77 per cent and 85 per cent of the corresponding Massachusetts rates. After 1920 the differentials suddenly increased, and the ratios between the various South Carolina rates and the comparable Massa-

TABLE 5

Wage Rates and Hours for Female Spinners and
Weavers in the Cotton Industry of Massachusetts
and South Carolina, 1890–1937*

| Year | Massachusetts | | | South Carolina | | |
| | Frame Spinners | | Weavers† | Frame Spinners | | Weavers† |
	Hours per Week	Rate per Hour	Rate per Hour	Hours per Week	Rate per Hour	Rate per Hour
1890..	60	$0.091	$0.119	66	$0.030	$0.062
1894..	55	.089	.121	66	.030	.057
1898..	58	.092	.125	66	.033	.060
1902..	58	.103	.137	66	.041	.068
1906..	58	.122	.156	65.7	.079	.099
1910..	56	.131	.150	60	.090	.122
1914..	53.9	.150	.168	60	.106	.130
1918..	53.7	.277	.303	56.5	.168	.200
1920..	47.9	.506	.548	54	.391	.468
1922..	48	.386	.415	54	.206	.260
1924..	48	.437	.487	55	.219	.299
1926..	48	.378	.420	55	.213	.276
1928..	48	.350	.405	55	.215	.277
1930..	48	.342	.415	54.8	.222	.312
1932..	48	.289	.336	55	.166	.262
1937..	35.1	.454	.523	33.7	.350	.486

* U. S. Bureau of Labor Statistics, *History of Wages in the United States from Colonial Times to 1928, with Supplement, 1929-1933,* Bulletin No. 604 (Washington: Government Printing Office, 1934), pp. 339-90, 395, 563, 564; data for 1937 from Beney, *op. cit.,* pp. 56, 59.

† Hours for weavers are practically identical with those for spinners.

chusetts rates from 1922 through 1928 ranged from 50 to 68 per cent. Since 1928 somewhat higher ratios have again prevailed. It is worthy of note that a wide differential existed in the 1920's just preceding and at the time of the loss of a large part of Lowell's cotton industry. The cotton manufacturers consulted are unanimously of the opinion that the differences in manufacturing costs between Massachusetts and the South brought about by higher wages, shorter hours, and various legislative restrictions applying to labor in Massachusetts were a factor of first importance in Lowell's loss of industry.

It has often been stated that southern labor is not actually cheaper than labor in New England because it is less efficient. Such statements are difficult to substantiate. They have not been made by any of the manufacturers consulted in connection with this study. In an average cotton mill, machine time controls production to so large an extent that opportunities for speeding or retarding production by minor differences in efficiency are small. An employer who has had experience with labor both in Lowell and in the South offers as his opinion that Lowell labor is more flexible and more adaptable and learns faster than southern labor; this, he makes plain, does not mean that one worker can operate more looms or spindles; in ordinary cotton manufacture adaptability is of less consequence than in various other industries. On the other hand,

the suggestion has been made by some manufacturers that the native workers of the South are
more readily teachable than foreign laborers because
of the difficulty which many of the foreigners experience in understanding English.

The question of what the bases are for the lower
wage scale of the South has no direct bearing upon
costs of manufacture; it is of consequence only that
the differential exists. However, in seeking the natural factors which have contributed to losses in the
cotton industry of New England, it is important to
know whether the wage differential which has
played so significant a role in these losses is based
upon natural environmental differences. Undoubtedly one factor in the low cost of labor in the Piedmont is the presence in the Piedmont and the
adjacent Appalachian valleys of numerous tenant
farmers and owners of poor highland farms accus-
tomed to a low standard of living and thus willing
to work for low wages. "A family wage of $30 or
more a week is sufficient to call from the farm thou-
sands of small owners whose vicissitudes with cotton, tobacco, or highland farming have left them
on the verge of failure." [1]

Cost of Living

Lower living costs in the South appear to be also
a factor in the lower wage rates, though the question

---

[1] R. B. Vance, *Human Geography of the South* (Chapel Hill: University of North Carolina Press, 1932), p. 295.

as to the extent to which the lower wages are compensated for by lower living costs is a much debated one. Two studies of cost of living recently made, one by the National Industrial Conference Board and one by the Social Research Division of the Works Progress Administration, result in closely similar conclusions as to relative costs in the East and South as compared with the United States as a whole. The measurement undertaken by these studies is not of differences in standard of living among the several areas but of differences in costs for a given standard. The indexes obtained by these investigations together with indexes of wages in the cotton industry in the East and South are shown in Table 6. The data indicate that costs of living in the South are relatively low, though not sufficiently low to account wholly for the wage differentials. Further data presented by the National Industrial Conference Board show that the greater savings in the South are in rent (Index 86) and in costs of fuel and light (Index 89.6).[1] Clothing costs are slightly below the average for the United States (Index 98.4), and food costs almost identical with the average for the country (Index 99.7).[2] The corresponding indexes for the East are rent, 107.5; fuel and light, 115.4; clothing, 100.6; food, 100.3.[3] The lower costs of housing, fuel, and clothing in the South undoubtedly bear some relation to climatic

---

[1] Beney, *op. cit.*, p. 202.   [2] *Ibid.*   [3] *Ibid.*

TABLE 6

Indexes of the Cost of Living of a Wage Earner's
Family in Several Geographic Regions Compared
With Indexes of Average Hourly and Weekly Earn-
ings of Male Workers in Cotton Manufacture*

Geographic Region	Cost of Living		Average Earnings	
	National Industrial Conference Board Index, March,1937†	Works Progress Administra-tion Index, March,1935	Index of Hourly Earnings, Sept., 1937	Index of Weekly Earnings, Sept., 1937
United States.	100.0	100.0	100.0	100.0
East§........	102.1	102.5	115.1	119.1
South........	96.5	96.7	92.6	90.9
Middle West .	98.7	101.4	.....	.....
Far West....	103.6	101.1	.....	.....

* *Ibid.*, pp. 13, 179, 180.
† Upkeep of automobile is included. Slightly different indexes
are given excluding this item.
§ In the "East" are included the New England states, New
York, New Jersey, and Pennsylvania.

differences. Rentals within a region vary greatly
with the size of the community, being, in general,
higher the larger the city.[1] In the saving of rent,
the fact that many of the cotton workers of the
South live in small communities is an important
factor.

While the South has an advantage over New

[1] *Ibid.*, p. 202.

England in its lower living costs, the present situation in Lowell as to food and housing costs appears to be a favorable one. In 1937 a study of relative living costs in thirty-eight cities widely distributed in the East, Middle West, Far West, and South, and varying greatly in size, was undertaken by the Albany Chamber of Commerce in co-operation with the Albany Business College. The survey dealt with three elements of living costs—food, housing, and "operating costs," which included electric and gas rates, telephone, water and tax rates. The cities were ranked on the basis of the relative costs in the various cities of each of the three items, the city ranked one having the *highest* and the one ranked thirty-eight the *lowest* costs. Lowell's score in this rating was: food, 25; housing, 38; operating costs, 7.[1] Thus, of the thirty-eight cities covered by the comparison, Lowell was reported to have the lowest housing costs. The relatively low rentals, of course, reflect the present lessened demand for space and cannot be assumed to have operated over any considerable period. While they last, however, they perhaps constitute an attraction to industrial enterprises. Some of the present manufacturers list relatively low cost of living among the advantages which Lowell offers as the location for their establishments.

---

[1] Information supplied by the Lowell Chamber of Commerce.

Taxes

In the costs of manufacturing, taxes have, of recent years, become an element of increasing importance and, in the years of depression, a factor with which many manufacturers in Lowell and elsewhere have found it difficult to cope. Taxes in Lowell are relatively high. Tax rates in the thirty-nine cities of Massachusetts in 1937 ranged from $28.40 per $1,000 of assessed valuation in Newton to $46.90 in Woburn. Lowell's rate was $42.80, the sixth highest in the state. It was exceeded by the rates of Newburyport, Chelsea, Somerville, Peabody, and Woburn. The rate, however, has little significance apart from the assessed valuations upon which it is levied. The complaint of many Lowell taxpayers is not only that the rate is high but that assessed valuations are excessive.

The difficult relief situation is an important factor in the high tax levy. The amount paid for public welfare in the city in 1937 was the equivalent of $18 per $1,000 of assessed valuation. Some of this came from state or federal sources, however, and the portion of the Lowell levy which was actually paid for relief was $12.98 per $1,000. This was the highest rate paid for this purpose in any city of Massachusetts.

Relatively high valuations arise in part from the recent prosperity of Lowell in contrast to its present depression. In the latter years of the World

War and the period immediately following (1918–
23), there was prosperity in response to the textile
"boom" which pervaded the country, and there was
justification for high valuations. The rapid defla-
tion of sale values and rentals in the period of industrial losses was accompanied by little decrease
in assessed valuations. That the total valuation of
the city has decreased, as shown in Table 7, is the
result, in considerable part, of demolition of property rather than of lowering of valuations, although
some substantial abatements have been secured by
manufacturers.

TABLE 7

Assessed Valuations and Tax Rates in Lowell,
1918–37

Year	Valuation	Tax Rate
1918	$ 98,774,850	$23.80
1920	123,803,827	27.20
1922	130,586,193	30.60
1924	140,531,320	29.40
1926	145,910,187	33.40
1928	136,675,260	28.40
1930	128,249,769	33.40
1932	116,977,606	42.00
1934	110,301,987	38.80
1936	104,349,850	46.40
1937	98,214,550	42.80

It is estimated by the secretary of the Taxpayers
Association that the present valuation should be
perhaps about $75,000,000 or $80,000,000.

Many charges are made of poor administration and wasteful use of public funds as factors which have contributed to high tax levies, though it is stated that recently progress has been made in curtailing the cost of government.

Some lightening of the tax burden was brought to manufacturers throughout Massachusetts in 1937 by the removal of machinery from the property subject to local taxation. It was formerly taxed at the same rate as real estate.

Tax comparisons even between cities of the same state are of doubtful significance because, while rates may be readily compared, the relation of assessed valuations to real values is a variable and intangible factor. Complaints of high taxes are widespread, though not universal, among manufacturers owning property in Lowell. It may be argued that it is merely human nature to regard taxes as too high. It seems significant, however, that in a similar investigation of Lawrence no complaint was received of excessive valuations and few complaints of a high tax rate (Lawrence rate in 1937— $36.80). Lawrence has had no cases before the state board which receives tax appeals. It seems probable that the tax situation in Lowell is a relatively unfavorable one as compared with the average for Massachusetts.

Satisfactory comparisons between Massachusetts and other states are impossible because of great diversity in the bases for taxation. New Hampshire, for example, has no state income tax, while Massachusetts has, but New Hampshire has a tax on "stock in trade," including machinery, raw stock, and finished products, and this of course will vary with the inventory at the time of levy. It is a well-known fact that many communities in the South offered tax exemption for varying periods as one attraction to factories, and also that many southern textile mills were originally, and some are still, outside corporate limits and free thus from municipal taxation; still others are in small municipalities where local taxes have been relatively low. It has been stated that in 1925 the "Massachusetts tax on cotton mills was forty per cent higher than in the Carolinas and sixty-six and two-thirds per cent higher than in Alabama and Georgia." [1] There seems no doubt that taxes upon textile mills in the South have in general been lower than in the long-established, densely settled manufacturing communities of Massachusetts and that tax differentials were a factor in the departure of textile mills from New England. It is also true that in recent years there has been a general increase of taxes in the South and that the differential tends to vanish. [2] One cotton company operating mills both in New England and the South describes present southern taxes as "not quite so high" as on its northern mill, and

---

[1] Robert Malcolm Keir, *Manufacturing* (New York: Ronald Press Co., 1928), p. 350.

[2] Lemert, *op. cit.*, pp. 107–10.

another states that the South's advantage in taxes is "largely disappearing."

The Cotton Industry

The history of Lowell's industries may now be reviewed in relation to these various factors. It has been shown (p. 103) that Lowell's cotton industry continued to expand until 1890. It will be seen from Table 8 that before that date Lowell had been surpassed as a cotton manufacturing center by Fall River, and that by 1899 a second rival, the city of New Bedford, had almost matched it in production. By 1919 both cities had far outstripped Lowell, Fall River's cotton manufactures having more than twice the value and New Bedford's nearly three times the value of those of Lowell. In subsequent years the industry declined sharply in each of the three cities, reaching minima in 1932, after which there was some revival. It will be seen that the decline was greatest proportionally in Lowell. Lowell lost 77 per cent of its workers in the cotton industry between 1919 and 1936, while Fall River lost 60 per cent and New Bedford 64 per cent. The loss for Massachusetts as a whole was 65 per cent. Lowell had 10.2 per cent of all the cotton workers in the state in 1919, 6.8 per cent in 1936.

During these same years Massachusetts was losing ground to rival states. In 1919, 28 per cent, by value, of all the cotton goods manufactured in the United States was made in Massachusetts. In 1935

TABLE 8

The Manufacture of Cotton Goods in Lowell, Fall River, and New Bedford*

	Value of Product in Millions of Dollars			Average Number of Wage Earners Employed		
	Lowell	Fall River	New Bedford	Lowell	Fall River	New Bedford
1875....	16.8	20.2	2.8	9,960	14,216	1,983
1890....	19.8	24.9	8.2	15,074	19,476	6,379
1899†...	17.0	29.3	16.7	13,730	26,465	12,286
1909†...	24.7	48.6	42.5	13,833	30,407	22,141
1914....	23.0	50.0	51.8	13,066	30,758†	28,719
1919....	60.4	135.8	177.1	12,479	31,805	35,206
1921....	26.9	67.9	89.8	10,639	28,454	28,505
1923....	39.0	100.9	120.5	11,683	30,774	31,955
1925....	28.6	79.4	109.6	8,773	24,773	29,891
1927....	18.9	66.7	93.5	6,758	25,552	29,079
1929....	12.5	56.3	86.2	4,135	19,628	25,784
1931....	4.7	27.6	43.0	2,391	13,255	17,702
1932....	4.1	17.2	23.5	1,900	9,328	11,719
1933....	6.3	26.3	36.2	2,488	13,638	17,027
1934....	6.7	31.4	41.3	3,004	15,605	18,003
1935....	7.3	31.6	33.4	3,059	13,047	13,091
1936....	7.0	29.1	30.8	2,878	12,867	12,685

* *Census of Massachusetts, 1875; Census of the United States,* 1890, 1910, 1920; Commonwealth of Massachusetts, *Statistics of Manufactures,* 1914, 1919, 1921; Commonwealth of Massachusetts, "Census of Manufactures" (Mimeographed reports issued annually and separately for each city, 1931-36; each annual report reviews the immediately past ten-year period for the major industries).

† Cotton small wares included.

the production of Massachusetts accounted for only 10.7 per cent of the country's total product. Massachusetts lost first place to North Carolina in 1926 and had yielded second place to South Carolina by 1929. While all of the New England states suffered serious losses, the losses in Massachusetts were greater proportionally than those in the other states. At the same time, cotton-goods manufacture in the country as a whole had shown decrease in value of products and numbers of workers; neither is, of course, an accurate index of volume of product. The loss in number of workers between 1919 and 1935 was approximately 14 per cent, that in value of products far greater because of the inflated prices of 1919.

It is thus apparent that in considering losses in value of products and numbers of workers in Lowell's cotton industry between 1919 and 1936 we are dealing with changes which in some measure affected totals for the country as a whole, but from which New England and especially Massachusetts suffered much more than did the industry as a whole, and which Lowell experienced even more severely than did its rival cities in the state.

Among factors creating difficulties for the cotton industry as a whole during this period, the competition of rayon and silk, which came to be devoted to various uses where cotton had previously held a monopoly, was one of major importance. Changing styles reduced the market for certain cotton

fabrics which had long been staples. Undoubtedly
some losses in numbers of workers were the result
of technological improvements and "stretchout"
systems which permitted decrease of numbers employed without decrease of product. After 1929
generally depressed conditions throughout the
country had their effect upon this industry as upon
most other industries.

The losses of New England in contrast to the
gains of the South must, of course, be explained on
other bases. The comparisons which have been made
point to the differentials in manufacturing costs
which have resulted from the South's lower wages,
longer hours, and fewer labor regulations as the
major factor in this loss. Lower living costs made
possible in part by climatic differences and in part
by the less densely settled character of the region
occupied have contributed to keeping southern
wages low. High taxes in the mature industrial
communities of New England in contrast to the
lower rates which have in general prevailed in the
more recently established manufacturing settlements of the Piedmont have increased the differential in manufacturing costs in favor of the South.

For some establishments in New England, though
not for those of Lowell, differentials in cost of
power may have been a minor factor, since, in general, purchased power is somewhat cheaper in the
Piedmont than in New England. Proximity to raw
materials, which undoubtedly was a factor of im-

portance in initiating cotton manufacture in the
Piedmont and in stimulating its development in earlier years, seems of recent years to have constituted
little advantage to the South and an advantage
which has probably been offset by that region's
greater distance from the primary cotton-goods
market.

The recency of establishment of many of the
southern factories constitutes in itself a factor favor-
ing the South, because the new factories have been
equipped in many cases with machinery improved
by the latest technological advances. The cotton
industry is so highly mechanized that the equipment of a cotton plant requires a large outlay of
capital. Exchange of old machinery for new is not
to be lightly undertaken. As New England mills,
in the period under discussion, reached a time when
replacement of equipment was needed, they could,
of course, replace it in New England, but, in view
of the difficulties which New England was experiencing from competition with the South, it might
be poor judgment to do so. The charge which is
frequently made that the cotton manufacturers of
New England have been negligent about keeping
their plants up to date may in some cases be justi-
fied, but in making this charge care should be taken
not to confuse negligence with the exercise of common sense.

An intangible factor, the significance of which,
if any, it is impossible to estimate, but which is pres-

ent in the minds of some manufacturers, is the
contrast in attitude toward manufacturing establishments which is said to differentiate southern communities from some northern manufacturing centers. Southern towns have in general welcomed the
mills and made definite efforts to attract them, while
in northern communities an attitude of hostility on
the part of press and public has sometimes been
apparent. It is probable that some residents of New
England's manufacturing towns, perceiving the sor-
did conditions which in the course of long industrial
history have too often come to be associated with
the mills, hold the manufacturers responsible for all
the ills of the community, forgetting that they are
also mainly responsible for the community's existence. There are indications that Lowell has not been
free from this error in logic.

That Massachusetts has suffered loss of more of
its cotton industry than have other New England
states must be laid, at least in part, it would seem,
to its stricter labor legislation; it is unfortunate
that the state has been forced to pay this penalty for
leadership in efforts toward social improvement. In
some cases, as compared with the less densely settled northern New England states, heavier taxation
in Massachusetts appears to have been a factor. A
cotton company which formerly operated one plant
in Lowell as well as one in Maine, and which consolidated its operations in Maine upon withdrawal
from Lowell, explains that the forty-eight-hour law

in Massachusetts and the higher taxes of Lowell were factors in its decision that greater economy of operation could be secured in Maine.

A comparison of Lowell with the cities of Fall River and New Bedford at once suggests Lowell's inland position as a factor in its greater losses. As has been shown, however, a possible saving of from ten to fifteen cents per hundredweight on the cost of cotton is an item of little significance. The cost of transporting fuel from the coast to Lowell constitutes an element of expense to which the seaboard cities are not subject. This was doubtless a factor in preventing Lowell's cotton industry from growing appreciably by the addition of mills dependent wholly upon steam power. It was logical that the mills which were water power owners should install steam equipment to supplement water power and should greatly increase their operations thereby. But when there were no more unused water-power sites at Lowell, new establishments planning to utilize steam power wholly naturally sought locations where cheaper fuel was obtainable. It is not surprising, therefore, that the cotton industries of Fall River and New Bedford continued rapid growth after Lowell's industry had become practically static. But it must be remembered that Lowell's cotton manufacturers enjoyed cheap water power, and the combined cost of water and steam power can scarcely have exceeded, and probably did not equal, the cost of steam power on the coast. Power costs, therefore, can hardly have been a factor in Lowell's greater loss of industry. In its supply of process water, Lowell was at no disadvantage; it had a distinct advantage over New Bedford. There remain as possible causes Lowell's relatively heavy taxes and the fact that all of its cotton plants were nearly a century old, though new units had repeatedly been added. There remains also an element of chance; Lowell's mills were few as compared with those of the two seaboard cities and, within so small a group, the laws of averages cannot be expected to work; the city may have happened to have slightly more than its proportionate share of mills in which the product manufactured was particularly subject to southern competition or to fashion changes, or in which management was, at the time, below the average in efficiency. Of the cotton companies which moved from Lowell or which ceased to manufacture between 1925 and 1931, the principal staple products had been cotton blankets, cotton flannels, ginghams, chambrays, shirtings, and, in one mill, wide sheeting. One company had added the manufacture of hosiery yarns and knitted underwear, and various adjustments to changing fashions had been undertaken as the market for ginghams waned. All of these staple products were subject to strong southern competition. On the other hand, corduroys and velveteens, the chief products of the Merrimack Company, products the converting of which is an elaborate process, have been slow to invade the

South. In 1927 New England was producing more than three times the yardage of plushes, velvets, and velveteens produced in the cotton states.[1] Moreover, from 1925 through 1930 a good market for corduroys and related fabrics provided by the automobile trade was an asset to manufacturers of these commodities. Similar factors in survival cannot be given in the case of the other remaining cotton corporation, whose chief lines of manufacture are among those in which the South is a strong competitor.

Woolen and Worsted Manufacture

The manufacture of woolen and worsted goods, like the cotton industry, is one in which numbers of workers and values of products in the United States declined sharply between 1923 and 1933, considerable losses occurring before the beginning of the general depression in 1929. The year 1923 was one of abnormally high production; however, a comparison of 1929 with any year between 1918 and 1923 shows a significant loss in number of workers. In contrast to the cotton industry, however, woolen and worsted manufacture did not lose ground in Massachusetts in competition with other states, and Lowell held a more important position within the state in this industry in 1933 and 1936 than in 1919 or 1923 (Table 9).

---

[1] U. S. Bureau of the Census, *Biennial Census of Manufactures, 1931* (Washington: Government Printing Office, 1935), pp. 230–231.

TABLE 9

Woolen and Worsted Manufacture in Lowell and in
Massachusetts, 1890–1936*

Year	Value of Products in Millions of Dollars		Average Number of Wage Earners Employed	
	Lowell	Massachusetts	Lowell	Massachusetts
1890....	3.5	57.7	2,074	31.834
1899†...	4.7	72.9	2,496	37,048
1909†...	6.1	140.7	3,049	53,195
1914....	3.9	127.4	1,916	53,377
1919....	9.8	342.6	1,925	53,864
1921....	8.1	262.6	1,938	56,644
1923....	11.2	352.1	2,303	64,842
1925....	11.0	280.0	2,129	54,876
1927....	9.8	268.8	1,988	51,064
1929....	9.3	242.9	2,102	45,673
1931....	6.5	147.7	1,751	37,221
1932....	3.9	87.8	1,327	28,593
1933....	7.3	148.8	1,977	39,808
1934....	5.9	125.7	1,662	35,991
1935....	10.0	193.9	2,466	49,416
1936....	11.7	209.8	2,560	48,421

* *Census of the United States*, 1890, 1910, 1920; Commonwealth of Massachusetts, *Statistics of Manufactures*, 1914, 1919, 1921; Commonwealth of Massachusetts, "Census of Manufactures," 1931-36 (Mimeographed reports).

† Felt goods included.

Massachusetts had approximately 32 per cent of the woolen and worsted industry of the country in 1919, the same percentage in 1933. Lowell had in 1919 2.8 per cent of the woolen and worsted industry of Massachusetts, measured by value of prod-

ucts, and 3.5 per cent measured by numbers
employed; in 1936 it had between 5 and 6 per cent
measured by either standard. The upswing in employment in woolen and worsted manufacture in
Lowell since 1932 restores the industry to the approximate level of employment which obtained in
1899 and in 1910,[1] before cessation of manufacture
by the Middlesex Company.

Lowell's increased relative importance in this
industry since 1919 results from the addition of several worsted manufacturing companies in the period
from 1918 to 1925. The closing years of the war
and the years immediately following constituted a
period of prosperity and expansion in the worsted
industry. which reached its climax in 1923. In these
years Lowell had available industrial space which
had been vacated by the Bigelow Carpet Company
and the United States Cartridge Company; it offered also skilled textile labor and was thus a natural choice of location for newly founded worsted
plants. Scarcely were the last of these companies
established when there began a serious slump in the
industry which greatly curtailed production. In the
course of this depression most of the woolen and
worsted companies which had been in operation in
Lowell before 1918 were eliminated. One sold out
to one of the new companies and the two plants were
consolidated. The new companies were strong con-

---

[1] Average number employed in 1910, 2,686.

cerns which succeeded in surviving the lean years.
There remain today the Massachusetts Mohair
Plush Company and the five worsted companies recently established. With the economic revival of
1935 and 1936, the worsted companies expanded
their production and the working of wool assumed
the leading place among Lowell's industries. One
effect of the changes has been the elimination of
the carded woolen industry, formerly represented
by the Middlesex Company and several smaller
establishments, and the concentration upon worsted
and mohair yarns and fabrics. This change is consistent with a general shift of emphasis from woolens to worsteds in the country as a whole in
accordance with changing fashions.

The question naturally arises as to why the woolen
and worsted industry has suffered no loss of relative importance in Massachusetts and in Lowell
while the cotton industry has declined so sharply.
Surely high labor costs and high taxes are of significance in this industry also. The answer appears
to be that they are not detrimental to the maintenance of an industry which is not confronted by
effective competition from regions having notably
lower costs. While there has been some development of the woolen and worsted industries in the
South, it is not yet sufficient to make that region
a serious competitor of New England. The cotton
industry of New England continued to grow after
the southern industry had equaled and surpassed it

in cotton consumption; the maximum cotton consumption in New England was in 1917, but New England was exceeded in cotton consumption by the South as early as 1905.[1] Not until the South had approximately equaled New England in spindleage did the actual decline of the cotton industry in New England begin.[2] The woolen and worsted industry in the South is very far from having reached this stage in competition.

But why has no effective competition developed? Why has the woolen and worsted industry not to a greater extent followed cotton in taking advantage of cheaper labor in the South? The following reasons have been given by woolen and worsted manufacturers who were asked this question. (1) Wool working has been more bound to sources of soft water than is cotton manufacture. Present devices for softening water, however, it is stated, go far toward eliminating this factor. (2) The warm climate of the South is ill suited for work in woolen mills. It is not clear that it is not equally ill suited for work in cotton mills. (3) The processes of woolen manufacture are somewhat more varied and intricate than those of cotton manufacture; it is hence more difficult to train raw labor for the industry. Though suggested by some manufacturers,

---

[1] U. S. Bureau of the Census, *Cotton Production and Distribution, 1927–28,* Bulletin 164 (Washington: Government Printing Office, 1928), p. 33.

[2] *Ibid.*

others doubt that this is a factor. (4) Boston is the principal market for raw wool. It is not clear that this would be more of a handicap to woolen mills in the South than the fact that all domestic cotton is produced in the South is to cotton mills in New England. (5) The tremendous investment in the North delays movement; it is very expensive to move, and northern manufacturers have been hoping for some regulation of labor which will give the North a better competitive chance. (6) The markets for woolens and worsteds are principally in the North; nearness to market is more important in the case of woolens and worsteds than in the case of cottons because in cotton goods there are more staple products and goods are sold in larger quantities; there are almost no staples in wool except serges and flannels, which, it is added, "nobody now buys"; in the marketing of fancy worsteds, close touch with changing styles and ability to deliver quickly are important factors. (7) The attraction of lower taxes, which helped to draw cotton mills to the South, is no longer operative to an important degree. Some manufacturers are of the opinion that the woolen and worsted industry will shift south increasingly, and others can see no reason why it has not done so earlier.

It seems probable that immediate access to sources of raw material was an important factor in *initiating* the cotton industry in the South and in stimulating its early growth. Once well established, it profited by low-priced labor and grew. It grew in a period of rapidly expanding industry when there was room for a cotton industry both in New England and the South; it grew before 1925 by the founding of additional establishments, in many cases by northern companies, rather than by the removal of cotton companies from New England to the South. To the woolen and worsted industry, the South, removed from primary markets both for raw material and finished product, did not offer the initial incentive which it offered to cotton, and the industry, which was prosperous in New England, was slow to experiment in new fields. The years since 1925, which have, for the most part, been years of difficulty for the industry in New England, have been also years when there was no room for expansion in this industry, and when growth in the South would have had to be accomplished chiefly by actual migration from New England. This, the heavy investment in New England resists. Recently, wage and tax differentials have been reduced and thus have constituted less attraction than formerly. Experiments in the manufacture of woolens and worsteds in the South are, however, going forward. The Uxbridge Worsted Company, which operates one plant in Lowell, has recently established a plant in Georgia.

In summary of the bases for the woolen and worsted industry in Lowell, it seems clear that, whereas the availability of Merrimack and Concord power was a major factor in initiating this manufacture, the greatest advantage which the city now offers to the industry is an excellent supply of experienced textile labor. An abundance of soft water is an asset to those of the worsted companies which use it for processing. Proximity to Boston and the possibility of quick transportation to New York are additional advantages. The supply of power at reasonable rates is a secondary factor; the industry uses Merrimack and Concord power in part, and in part power supplied by the Lowell Electric Light Corporation. Availability of industrial space for purchase or rental at moderate rates was an incentive in the establishment of several of the present companies.

The Knit-Goods Industry

The knit-goods industry profits from essentially the same advantages. It is a venerable industry in Lowell, though statistics for it are fragmentary, separate data having been published only intermittently. In 1864 the Lawrence Manufacturing Company added to the production of cotton cloth the manufacture of knitted stockings and underwear.[1] The Lowell Hosiery Company was founded in 1869 and the Shaw Stocking Company was established in Lowell in 1877 to manufacture the seamless stockings for which Benjamin Shaw had

---

[1] Stone, *op. cit.*, I, 737.

invented the machinery.[1] These two companies occupied sites which afforded no access to water
power, and it is probable that their choice of Lowell
as a location was based upon the labor supply and
other advantages afforded by a long-established
textile community. In 1890 the hosiery and knit
goods produced in Lowell had a value of $731,413.[2]
By 1905 the value of product had increased to
nearly $4,000,000 and more than 4,000 workers
were employed.[3] In 1919 the industry was represented by five establishments employing 5,357 workers and producing goods with a value of $17,172,-
099.[4] This amount constituted about one-third the
value of all the knit goods produced in Massachusetts.[5]

Since 1919 there have been many changes in the
industry; old companies have gone, new ones have
come, and the net result is a larger number of establishments than in 1919 but fewer workers and a
smaller fraction of the total knit-goods product for
the state produced in Lowell. In 1936, 2,710 workers were employed; products were valued at $7,433,-
200, which constituted 21.4 per cent of the total for
Massachusetts. Changes have also involved a shift

---

[1] F. W. Coburn, *History of Lowell and Its People* (New York:
Lewis Historical Publishing Co., 1920), I, 356.

[2] *Eleventh Census of the United States: 1890*, Vol. VI, *Manufacturing Industries*, Part II, p. 317.

[3] *Census of Massachusetts, 1905*, III, 101.

[4] Commonwealth of Massachusetts, *Statistics of Manufactures, 1919*,
p. 23.

[5] *Ibid.*, p. 6.

in emphasis from seamless cotton hosiery and cotton underwear, which constituted much of the output of earlier years, to outerwear, knitted fabrics, and hosiery of other types, involving the use of a variety of textiles.

The knit-goods industry is one in which, in contrast to cotton and woolen manufacture, the total number of workers in the United States increased between 1919 and 1929; there were, however, as in cotton, important shifts in distribution, New England's industry decreasing in absolute importance and that of the Middle Atlantic states in relative importance, while the South made large gains in both.[1] These gains were chiefly in the cotton and rayon hosiery and cotton underwear branches of the industry, the manufacture of knitted cloth and knitted outerwear invading the South but little.[2] The production of seamless hosiery and of the heavier grades of cotton underwear have almost disappeared from New England. The bases for gains in these types of manufacture in the South and losses in New England and in Lowell are identical with those for similar shifts in the distribution of cotton manufacture. In other branches of the knit-goods industry, New England's competition has been chiefly with the

[1] U. S. Bureau of the Census, *Location of Manufactures* (Washington: Government Printing Office, 1933), pp. 18–19.

[2] U. S. Bureau of the Census, *Fifteenth Census of the United States: 1930. Manufactures, 1929*, Vol. II (Washington: Government Printing Office, 1933), pp. 301–3, 306–7.

Middle Atlantic states,[1] which have long been lead-
ers in the knit-goods industry as a whole. In these
fields New England finds it easier to compete, since
the Middle Atlantic states constitute a region of
relatively high wage scales. Changes in the general
character of the knit-goods industry in Lowell have
thus been in accord with the general nature of
changes elsewhere in New England. Losses have
been greater than in Massachusetts as a whole, perhaps because of the previous emphasis in Lowell
upon those phases of the industry which were most
subject to southern competition and which were also
affected by general decline of market as a result of
changing fashions. While losses in the knit-goods
industry in Lowell have apparently been due to the
same factors as loss of cotton manufacture, the
decline has been less serious than might otherwise
have been the case, for the very reason that the space
and power available in the vacated cotton mills have
helped to attract new knitting companies to Lowell.
All but one of the knitting plants now in Lowell
occupy space in former cotton mills.

The Rayon Industry

The rayon industry in Lowell is wholly the out-
growth of the period of transition since 1918. The
Newmarket Manufacturing Company was formerly
a manufacturer of cotton goods, but before its re-

---

[1] *Ibid.;* U. S. Bureau of the Census, *Biennial Census of Manufactures, 1931,* pp. 269–70.

moval to Lowell (p. 109) it had foreseen the future difficulties of the New England cotton industry and had shifted to the manufacture of silk and rayon. The removal from Newmarket was prompted by temporary difficulties in the labor situation there, and Lowell was chosen as the new location because of the labor supply and the industrial space which it offered. Silk manufacture was later discontinued. The Wannalancit Company was founded in Lowell following the removal of cotton corporations and occupies space in the plant of the Appleton Company. A good labor supply and quick access to the New York market are the chief advantages which Lowell offers to these companies. They make no use of process water and they are not near sources of raw material (p. 137). Competition with the South is vigorous. The representative of one company states that, in the case of any new equipment going into the industry, other labor markets would have to be considered.

Cotton Small Wares

Of the lesser textile industries, the manufacture of cotton small wares, including narrow fabrics and elastic cords and webbing, is an industry which has shown gains in Massachusetts and in Lowell since 1919. Lowell accounted for about 4.6 per cent of the state's product in this industry in 1919,[1] about

---

[1] Commonwealth of Massachusetts, *Statistics of Manufactures, 1919*, pp. 4, 23.

6 per cent in 1936. The number of workers in this industry in Lowell in 1936 (p. 33) was more than double the number in 1919.[1] The industry is one of much more recent development in New England than the cotton-goods industry.[2] Of the six companies in Lowell covered by the statistics for this industry in 1936, all but one have been established since 1915. There were, however, some earlier companies which are no longer present. The industry is also one in which the South, so far as the latest available census figures show, has as yet offered no effective competition.[3]

The companies manufacturing shoe bindings, shoelaces, and industrial tapes and webbings state that central position with relation to the New England market is an advantage, or the major advantage, which Lowell offers to them. Low rent and abundant labor are given by several companies as advantages. Other favorable factors mentioned by one or more companies are reasonable power rates, good transportation, and low cost of living. One company is just now leaving the city to consolidate with another firm operating under more favorable conditions; it reports that taxes and the costs of labor and power are higher in Lowell than in some other cities engaged in similar manufacture; this

---

[1] *Ibid.*, p. 23.

[2] Artman, *op. cit.*, p. 329.

[3] U. S. Bureau of the Census, *Biennial Census of Manufactures, 1931*, p. 246.

company was not within the Merrimack or Concord power area.

Other Textile Industries

The companies making insulated wire were both founded before 1919. Their reports indicate that they now find no bases for location in Lowell except abundant labor and the fact that they are already established and operating there. Their markets are chiefly outside New England, and the yarns used by the larger company come chiefly from the South. Several small-scale textile manufacturers located in buildings once used for cotton manufacture also note the abundance of experienced labor and, in addition, low costs of rent and power as advantages which Lowell offers to their industries.

The present companies handling cotton waste were founded before 1923 and one goes back to 1893. The apparent basis for location in Lowell was the presence there of an important cotton industry. One waste company was eliminated in the period during which the number of cotton mills was greatly reduced. Now most of the stock processed by the remaining companies comes from outside sources, much of it from the South. Under these circumstances Lowell offers little advantage to such an industry except plentiful labor and low rentals. One company is now liquidating its stock.

Another branch of textile manufacture which has

been affected adversely by the decline of the cotton
industry is the bleaching, dyeing, and finishing of
textiles. Much of this work was done in the mills
of the cotton and woolen manufacturers, but separate establishments engaged in the industry appeared early in the history of the city, the Lowell
Bleachery having been incorporated in 1832. Between 1920 and 1923 there were, excluding the
textile manufacturers, seven establishments engaged
in this industry; the annual product ranged in value
between $5,000,000 and $10,000,000, and more than
1,000 workers were employed.[1] Only one of these
companies now remains in Lowell, the Waterhead
Mills, corduroy converters (p. 37). One company,
dyeing and printing wool tops, has moved to a location in Dracut shortly beyond the boundary of
Lowell. Of the five which have discontinued operations or moved to more distant locations, four were
bleachers and dyers of cotton, three handling cotton cloth and one cotton yarns; one company dyed
and finished worsteds and woolens. Most of the
removals occurred between 1925 and 1931. Statistics have not since been published separately for the
industry. It is not discoverable to what extent these
former companies derived their business from
Lowell manufacturers; in any case the removal of
the bleachers and dyers of cottons is undoubtedly

[1] Commonwealth of Massachusetts, *Statistics of Manufactures, 1920,*
p. 24; *1921,* p. 26; U. S. Bureau of the Census, *Biennial Census of Manufactures, 1923* (Washington: Government Printing Office, 1926), p. 1420.

associated with the decline of the cotton industry in New England.

In addition to the corduroy-converting company, the dyeing and finishing industry in Lowell is now represented by a company established in 1933 in one of the former cotton mills, which dyes yarns, narrow fabrics, and hosiery. A large percentage of its work is done for Lowell manufacturers, and proximity to customers is the major advantage which the city offers to it. This company uses Merrimack water and the corduroy-converting company Concord water for processing.

The company engaged in scouring and carbonizing wool chose Lowell as the location for its factory because of unexcelled water for its purposes, proximity to Boston, and availability in the plant of the Middlesex Company of industrial space with partial equipment for the wool-scouring industry. The company indicates that if the same water were available nearer Boston such a location would be still more favorable, since Boston is the chief source of its raw material. Little of its business is derived from Lowell.

Foundry and Machine-Shop Products

Associated in its development with the textile industries was the manufacture of textile machinery and parts and textile machine repair work. This industry was initiated promptly after the establishment of the Merrimack Company by the construction of the machine shop in which was built much of the machinery for the mills which followed. The immediate local demand for the product was clearly the primary reason for the foundation of this industry. When the era of rapid textile mill building in Lowell had come to an end, the Lowell Machine Shop had won a sufficient reputation that its products were widely sought in other places. Its markets expanded and the industry grew. Also there had been developed in Lowell a body of labor experienced in the machinery trades, which, together with such demand for machinery and machine parts and repairs as the Lowell mills still provided, doubtless encouraged the founding in Lowell of other establishments engaged in the manufacture and repair of textile machinery. Other machinery trades appear also to have been attracted by Lowell's skilled mechanics and by the demands of a city in which varied industries were gradually developing. Foundry work was of course, in turn, needed to supply the demands of the machinery trades.

In 1890 and for many years thereafter the manufacture of foundry and machine-shop products including textile machinery and parts ranked third among the city's industries, exceeded only by cotton and woolen and worsted manufacture. In most years from 1890 to 1922, between 2,000 and 3,000 workers were employed. In 1923 there were 3,228 workers in the industry and the value of its products amounted to $8,073,816.[1] A marked recession began in the following year in coincidence with the textile depression of 1924. It continued until 1932, when the number of workers was 153 and the value of products less than $500,000.[2] Since then there has been revival, as shown by the figures for 1936 (p. 33). Production in this industry in Massachusetts has fallen and risen since 1923 in sympathy with the fluctuation in Lowell, but the net loss in Lowell was much greater. Lowell accounted for about 12 per cent (13 per cent by numbers employed; 11 per cent by value) of the state's production in 1923, scarcely more than 2 per cent in 1936.

A large part of the decrease in Lowell was the result of the removal of the Saco-Lowell Shops (p. 105), by far the largest establishment for machinery manufacture in the city. Cessation of demand, as a result of drastic changes in the textile industry, for the types of machinery manufactured in the Lowell plant, while the market for the products of the company's Biddeford plant continued, is given as a reason for the decision to consolidate operations in Biddeford and Saco. The company states that high taxes were also a factor in its withdrawal from Lowell.

Some smaller establishments have ceased opera-

---

[1] U. S. Bureau of the Census, *Biennial Census of Manufactures, 1923*, p. 1420.
[2] Commonwealth of Massachusetts, "Census of Manufactures, 1936 —City of Lowell," p. 4.

tions, including two foundries, but the total number of plants has been little reduced. Further decreases in production after the withdrawal of the Saco-Lowell Shops appear to have been due chiefly to a lowering of the product per company. Most of the present companies, replying to a question as to the advantages which Lowell offers to this industry, reply that it offers none. One manufacturer of textile machinery states that central position in the largest market area for the company's products constitutes an advantage. As disadvantages are cited the decrease of demand owing to loss of industries and, repeatedly, high taxes. One company complains of high freight rates, one of high power rates, and one of position "off the main line."

It seems clear that although this industry, initially founded upon local demand, had come to have wide external markets, the local market was still sufficiently important to some branches of the trade so that the decrease of manufacturing in Lowell meant a serious loss. This was especially true of companies engaged in textile machine repair work. To some companies, the decline of textile manufacture in New England as a whole was significant; even establishments having their chief markets outside New England were affected by the depression and the shifting character of production in the textile industries following 1923, or the general economic depression following 1929. The majority of the companies in this industry in Lowell occupy separate buildings outside the central mill ring in which special advantages of rent and power have recently been offered. Raw materials used in the industry are heavy in proportion to value and their ultimate sources well removed. As markets for the products of the industry move increasingly to distant areas, it is natural that some manufacturers of these products should seek in vain for advantages which location in Lowell offers to them. Most of the present companies are old and the resistance of established industry to change helps to preserve the portion of this branch of manufacture which remains.

Shoe Manufacture

Shoe manufacture is one of the most mobile of industries. Shifts in the location of establishments are frequent, and the chief basis for migration is usually the seeking of more advantageous labor markets. The mobility of the industry results from the average smallness of scale of individual establishments, the fact that machinery is leased rather than purchased, that space is very often rented rather than owned, and that, therefore, the amount of capital invested is small in relation to the value of the product. An incentive to move is provided by recurrent labor agitation resulting in part from the high degree of organization of labor in this industry. The development of powerful labor organizations is, in turn, favored by the concentration of the industry in certain centers, the strong competi-

tion between the many small establishments, which
tends to retard close co-operation between employers, and the fact that the "employers in the
shoe industry as a class are not fortified by large
masses of capital."[1] Not only is the industry mobile, but it is one in which both the birth rate and
the mortality are very high. Because of the ease
with which operations can be initiated, many companies are founded without adequate financial back-
ing and are soon eliminated by the keen competition
of their rivals. Moreover, the constant changes of
style in women's shoes contribute to making the
risks involved in manufacture excessive.[2]

As a result of these various factors, fluctuations
in the industry in any community may bear little
relation to general trends in the region of which it
is a part. A shoe manufacturer may move into a
city in which there is little or no shoe industry and,
of course, no organization of labor in the industry,
seeking relief from labor agitation and lower labor
costs than those to which he has been subject in the
shoe center in which he has previously been located.
He finds them and is perhaps able to undersell his
competitors. His success attracts others. Competition in the labor market ensues and the cost of
labor rises. Unionization follows and costs rise further. The advantage in labor costs vanishes. Some
companies move on or are extinguished in the

---

[1] Keir, *op. cit.*, p. 462.　　　　[2] *Ibid.*, p. 469.

TABLE 10

Boot and Shoe Manufacture in Lowell, Haverhill, and Massachusetts, 1890–1936*

Year	Value of Product in Millions of Dollars			Average Number of Wage Earners Employed		
	Lowell	Haver-hill	Massa-chusetts	Lowell	Haver-hill	Massa-chusetts
1890....	0.07	19.5	116.4	98	12,087	69,934
1895....	.84	16.0	104.6	499	6,512	54,056
1899....	.97†	19.5	117.1	517†	8,323	58,645
1904....	1.5 †	20.5§	144.3	819†	7,802§	62,633
1909....	2.7 †	29.1	187.0	1,259†	9,603	74,710
1914....	3.5	35.6	200.5	1,485	11,172	76,944
1919....	3.1	59.7	442.5	674	11,529	80,166
1922....	2.5	34.1	276.2	702	8,994	70,294
1924....	4.3	28.5	246.9	1,223	8,043	62,969
1926....	4.5	31.9	244.2	1,277	8,350	59,738
1928....	8.3	25.0	238.9	2,119	6,467	55,478
1930....	8.2	18.8	185.1	2,390	5,394	49,105
1931....	8.0	15.5	160.7	2,992	4,639	47,634
1932....	5.8	13.3	126.2	2,379	4,873	43,265
1933....	3.7	14.7	128.0	1,632	5,820	46,739
1934....	4.5	14.2	134.0	1,640	5,198	45,951
1935....	4.3	11.8	132.7	1,706	4,880	44,371
1936....	5.4	11.5	142.3	1,892	4,522	46.294

* *Census of the United States*, 1890, 1900, 1910; *Census of Massachusetts*, 1895, 1905; Commonwealth of Massachusetts, *Statistics of Manufactures*, 1909, 1914, 1919; Commonwealth of Massachusetts, "Census of Manufactures," 1931-36 (Mimeographed reports).

† Cut stock and findings included.

§ 1905.

struggle for existence; the shoe industry in the community declines.

Two such cycles are apparent in the history of the industry in Lowell, as shown by the data in Table 10. Shoe manufacture was of little consequence in the city before 1890. At about that time several companies moved from Haverhill, attracted by favorable labor conditions. As has been shown, wages in the cotton industry average lower than those in shoe manufacture, thus creating a favorable labor market for the more highly paid industry. The industry enlarged gradually until the years of the World War. Then the rapid expansion of the United States Cartridge Company, which offered high wages, and of other industries stimulated by the war tended to absorb shoe workers; conditions for the industry became difficult and there was a marked recession. The decline in the cotton industry and other associated manufactures following 1923 created again a favorable labor market. Also rent and power at low rates became available. The industry rose rapidly, reaching the climax of its development (as measured by numbers employed) in 1931, when most industries were greatly depressed. In that year shoe manufacture was the city's leading industry. The resultant increased demand for labor within the industry, coupled with that occasioned by the partial revival of other industries after 1932, tended to destroy special advantages and a second recession occurred.

It will be seen by comparing data for Lowell with those for the neighboring shoe city of Haverhill that the industry suffered losses in Haverhill between 1890 and 1905 when it was beginning its rise toward importance in Lowell, and that it was declining in Haverhill between 1924 and 1931 at the time when it was rising to its second climax in Lowell. The number of shoe manufacturing establishments in Haverhill decreased from 172 in 1923 to 91 in 1931, while in Lowell the number rose from 7 to 15. Decentralization was at work in the long-established shoe center, a change from which Lowell, in some measure, profited. In Massachusetts the industry receded from 1919 to 1923 as in Lowell, but in the state the recession continued until 1932 with no revival in the later twenties coincident with that in Lowell. During these years until 1929 the industry was growing in various states, mainly in the interior, at the expense of Massachusetts. It seems clear that the special local circumstances described were responsible for the rise of the industry in Lowell in the years following 1923.

Present shoe manufacturers in Lowell appear to be more conscious of competition with New Hampshire and Maine than with states in the interior, probably because the markets of their New England neighbors are more nearly identical with their own. Lower labor costs in these states and a longer working day in Maine are named as factors which make successful competition difficult.

Apart from labor factors, shoe manufacturers mention suitable manufacturing space, nearness to Boston, convenient shipping facilities, and favorable power rates as circumstances which led to their location in Lowell.

The shoe industry in New England, in contrast with the textile industries, has been little associated with sites where water power was available. This is doubtless the result of the relative lateness of invention of most of the machinery used in shoe manufacture. The more accessible power sites had been occupied by the textile industries before the widespread introduction of power-driven machinery in shoe manufacture had made these sites significant to producers of shoes. Shoe manufacture, long a cottage and workshop industry, tended to become concentrated in towns where there were no large-scale textile industries to give employment to local labor. Hence the small importance of the industry in Lowell before 1890. Shoe manufacturers recently established in Lowell take advantage of the late opportunity, not now of much significance, to utilize the water power no longer monopolized by the textile industries.

Manufacturers of boot and shoe "cut stock and findings" find Lowell in a convenient location for the distribution of their products to the New England shoe trade.

Other Industries

The many other industries of Lowell appear to be based for the most part upon advantages which the city offers to industry in general rather than upon special advantages for particular industries; or they are based upon conditions provided by cities in general rather than by Lowell in particular—that is, upon a local market for their products such as would be provided as well by any city having within its tributary area a population of similar numbers, tastes, and buying power. In the latter class belong many establishments in the printing, newspaper-publishing, baking, bottling, ice cream, confectionery, lumber-working, and stone-working trades. It has been seen, however, (pp. 43, 44, 46, 143) that some establishments belonging to this group of trades command considerable external markets; these owe their location in Lowell to other advantages which the city offers to industry, rather than to the local market.

The factors cited by the greatest numbers of manufacturers in miscellaneous trades (eliminating those dependent wholly upon local markets) as contributing to make Lowell a satisfactory location for their industries are low rents, abundant labor, and good transportation facilities. Relatively low cost of living, low power costs, skilled labor, nearness to Boston, and quick access to New York are also repeatedly named. A few indicate relatively

low-priced labor for their industries and a few con-
cede reasonable taxes.

Among these varied industries, the manufacture
of paper boxes, tubes, and other paper products is
one which has of late years assumed considerable
proportions, replacing in importance the manufacture of wooden boxes in earlier years. The enlargement appears to be due chiefly to general growth
in this industry rather than to conditions pertaining
particularly to Lowell. The great increase in and
enormous variety of uses to which the products of
this industry are put furnish a basis for enlargement. The textile manufacturers of Lowell provide
some market for the textile winding cores which are
one of the products of this industry, but a small
market in proportion to the total product.

The manufacture of patent medicines has taken
a prominent place in Lowell's industrial history.
In 1890 the value of the products of the industry
exceeded $2,000,000, 461 workers were employed,[1]
and the city had the reputation of being the leading
city of the country in this branch of manufacture.
As late as 1921 the value of products was more
than $1,000,000.[2] In recent years separate statis-
tics for the industry have not been published. It
was founded in 1843 when J. C. Ayer began the

---

[1] *Eleventh Census of the United States: 1890,* Vol. VI, *Manufacturing Industries,* Part II, pp. 315, 317.

[2] Commonwealth of Massachusetts, *Statistics of Manufactures, 1921,*
p. 26.

preparation and sale of "Cherry Pectoral."[1] Later, the C. I. Hood Company established large laboratories for the manufacture of various patent preparations. Other establishments followed. The very large-scale advertising done by the Ayer Company, which in 1898 was printing almanacs in eighteen languages, was a factor in the establishment in Lowell of the Lowell Electrotype Foundry.[2] No environmental factors can be cited as having given any special advantage to this industry. The largest two concerns were founded by men who had had experience in Lowell's apothecary shops. The Hood Company has discontinued operations in Lowell (plant recently occupied by the Hatch Paper Box Company and now partially vacant, p. 114); the Ayer Company and Carleton and Hovey, manufacturers of "Father John's Medicine," remain. A change in the public attitude toward patent medicines has probably been responsible for decrease in this industry.

The growth of varied industries began early in Lowell's history, stimulated doubtless by the labor supply assembled by the textile industries, the good transportation facilities, and the markets provided by the growing settlement. In 1880 cotton goods still accounted for more than half the value of all the products of the city's industries; in 1923 they constituted 39 per cent of the total product by value.

---

[1] Coburn, *op. cit.,* I, 246.

[2] *Lowell Courier Citizen, op. cit.,* p. 33a.

It will be seen from Table 1 (p. 33) that in 1936
the miscellaneous industries for which data are not
separately given supplied more than one-third of
the city's total industrial product.

Summary

In summary, it appears that Lowell is not subject to any environmental handicaps which are not
common to inland New England cities. Like all
New England, it is removed from the primary
sources of the chief primary raw materials and, with
the movement of settlement westward, it has been
left remote from the center of the country's population. A seaboard city such as Boston has an advantage in obtaining fuel and some raw materials
at lower cost and in the shipment of finished products by water. Not every seaboard city, however,
is provided with adequate shipping services. An
inland position near Boston and hence near the terminals of many steamship lines probably offers
greater transportational advantages than a position
on the northern portion of the New England coast.
In the case of certain products, position in New
England has not prevented Lowell's retention of
distant markets which theoretically might well have
been seized by areas nearer both to raw materials
and to those markets; Lowell manufacturers have,
for example, important markets for worsted goods
and shoes in the Middle West. While some of the
city's former establishments did not compete suc-

cessfully with the South in cotton manufacture, remoteness from the source of raw material appears to have been a factor of little significance in this failure. However, remoteness from markets and raw materials undoubtedly tends in some cases to make competition with other industrial areas more difficult and to increase the risks of manufacturing.

While Lowell is as well favored as most New England cities, it does not now have the outstanding advantages which it once enjoyed. Its natural power resource is no longer the great asset which it once was, since modern power developments have made electric power so widely available and at so little variation in cost from place to place. In its early days its natural location, together with the stimulus to the development of transportation which the early establishment of industries there provided, combined to give it exceptional facilities for transportation. Such advantages as to rail transportation are now more common, and the extensive use of trucking detracts from the significance of positions at rail foci. Access to soft water is still an asset in certain industries, but the ability to obtain it by chemical treatment of hard water lessens the importance of the possession of this asset. Nearness to Boston is less an advantage than in the days of less rapid transportation.

As environmental features assume less importance, man-made ones increase in significance in influencing the distribution of industry. In efficient

government and economical administration, Lowell
appears on the whole to have been less fortunate
than many Massachusetts cities. In common with
many other New England cities, Lowell is a
mature industrial community in which the advantages inherent in a fresh start in manufacturing,
and in less highly organized community life, are
lacking.

In common with all Massachusetts and to a
lesser degree all New England, Lowell suffers in
competition with regions of lower wage scales and
less stringent labor regulations. It was unfortunate in having as its major industry, contributing
in 1923 nearly 40 per cent of the total value of its
manufactured products, an industry particularly
subject to competition from such a region, and in
having also other important industries dependent
in large part upon the prosperity of the New England cotton industry. Thus it has suffered more
severely than most New England industrial cities.
Loss of industry in turn may have helped to breed
further losses through increasing tax levies upon
remaining manufacturers, though at the same time
it made space and power available for the introduction of new companies. A psychological factor may
tend to retard the movement of new industries into
a city which is known to have suffered severe industrial losses. It appears that in the interplay of these
various factors are to be found the bases for Lowell's
industrial rise and decline.

CHAPTER 5

Future Possibilities

LOWELL'S FUTURE, like its past, is in part
dependent upon factors affecting all New England; it is in part dependent upon circumstances
within the city itself. Will the migration of the
textile industries from North to South continue,
woolen and worsted manufacture and the branches
of the knit-goods industry which are still en-
trenched in the North moving southward in the
wake of cotton? If so, Lowell faces the necessity
for further grave industrial readjustments.

In answer to this question it can only be said
that the advantages which the South has thus far
offered are partly of an impermanent character.
It is obvious that no factory and no community can
long remain young. Maturity with its attendant
disadvantages will overtake the South's industrial
settlements in time. It has been indicated that tax
differentials between New England and the South
are diminishing, as seems inevitable if roads, schools,
and municipal services are to be improved in a
measure consistent with the South's industrial
growth. As industrial communities increase in size,
costs of living tend to increase, creating demands
for higher wages. When the workers have been

longer dissociated from the rural backgrounds from which they came, their insistence upon higher rates of pay seems probable.

Opinions differ widely as to the capacity of labor organizations to bring about higher wage rates in the South. One opinion is that "unionization . . . seems powerless at this stage to cope with the excess labor supply that besieges factory doors as potential strike breakers." [1] On the other hand, representatives of two manufacturing companies operating mills both in New England and the South who were consulted testify that, in the area in which their southern mills are located, labor has of late been very insistent in its demands and that the results have practically eliminated the greater profits formerly obtained from their southern mills. One manufacturer describes southern labor organization as now experiencing the "growing pains" and attendant stimulus to "unreasonable" demands which in the North have long since been suffered and survived.

Federal legislation will perhaps be a powerful factor in decreasing wage differentials, though there is no certainty to what extent such a reduction will be permanently accomplished by the mere establishment of minimum wage rates. State legislation constitutes also a potential factor. In view of the various forces at work toward increasing wages in the

---

[1] Vance, *op. cit.*, p. 296.

South, it seems probable that regional wage differentials will tend to decrease. In so far, however, as the lower costs of living in the South result from climatic factors, they justify the permanent maintenance of a wage differential. This would probably not be great enough to constitute an important stimulus to industrial migration; it will be remembered that the index of weekly earnings in the southern cotton industry obtained by an investigation in 1937 was 28.2 lower in the South than in the East, while the index of cost of living was only 5.6 lower (p. 166).

A smoothing out of regional cost differentials will scarcely return to New England the portion of the cotton industry which it has lost, but it may prevent the further extensive migration of industry. However, New England's best chances for success would seem to be in industries in which it could capitalize its long industrial experience—in the making of products which do not admit of large-scale standardized production—products in the manufacture of which experience, versatility, and adaptability of labor are more important than cheapness, and in the marketing of which it is possible to maintain a wider spread than in staple standardized products between the cost of raw materials and the price of the finished product. Also emphasis should be upon industries in which the costs of transportation of raw materials and of sending finished products to market constitute an insignificant element in total costs; this situation may result from the fact that sources of materials, or principal markets, or both, are near at hand, or that the goods transported have high value in proportion to bulk and weight.

If Lowell is to have the share of the industry of New England to which its natural advantages entitle it, its immediate problems are those of reducing dependence upon relief, lowering taxes, and matching its expenditures to its lowered assets. Toward the reduction of relief, continuance of the progress which has been made in replacing old industries by new ones is of the utmost significance. It has been shown that there is further industrial space available. As for water power, it is reported that with the upturn of industry in the winter and spring of 1937 the amount of Locks and Canals water used at any one hour was between two-thirds and three-fourths of the maximum use in 1920, but that since second shifts were common in 1937, as they were not in 1920, the actual total use of water was not very different from that in 1920. With the recession of the latter half of 1937 and 1938 the amount used was greatly reduced. It is apparent that, at least upon a single-shift basis, there is room for more industries using Merrimack power. This can of course be supplemented with power from other sources at times of low water or of abnormal demand. If the city hopes to contribute to the solution of its problems through increasing employment, it will presumably offer every reasonable encouragement to industry to utilize its remaining industrial space and power.

If such encouragement does not succeed, the alternative is to secure balance in other ways between the population of the community and its population-supporting capacity. Such adjustment has of course been delayed by general lack of prosperity in the country as a whole. When unemployment was widespread, there was no incentive for the unemployed to move from Lowell to other areas where there were also unemployed. But such lack of balance cannot continue indefinitely without meaning further loss of industry. To continue to tax present industries with the burdens imposed by loss of former ones tends obviously toward increasing the acuteness of the problem. It is recognized that the problem is a circular one and difficult of solution.

In common with most industrial cities, Lowell has areas where slum clearance and the substitution of decent living quarters are sorely needed. This will bear investigation as a possible field in which federal funds available for work projects might be employed.

It is clear that Lowell may emerge from its crisis a smaller city. The goal to be sought is not restoration to former size, but the best possible utilization of the opportunities offered, so as to secure the maximum advantage to as large a population as can be adequately supported. The attainment of this goal will require the cooperation of Lowell's citizens—the coordinated efforts of city officials and taxpayers, of wage earners and employers—of all who are concerned for the future welfare of the city.

BIBLIOGRAPHY

ALLEN, WILKES. *The History of Chelmsford.* Haverhill: P. N. Green, 1820.

American Wool and Cotton Reporter, July 23, 1925 (vol. not numbered), pp. 228–35; XLII (April 7, 1938), 58.

American Geographical Society. *New England's Prospect.* Edited by John K. Wright. New York, 1933.

APPLETON, NATHAN. *Introduction of the Power Loom and the Origin of Lowell.* Lowell: B. H. Penhallow, 1858.

ARTMAN, C. E. *Industrial Structure of New England.* U. S. Department of Commerce, Domestic Commerce Series, No. 28. Washington: Government Printing Office, 1930.

——. *New England's Manufactures in the Nation's Commerce.* U. S. Department of Commerce, Trade Information Bulletin No. 582. Washington: Government Printing Office, 1928.

BENEY, M. A. *Differentials in Industrial Wages and Hours in the United States.* National Industrial Conference Board Studies, No. 239. New York: National Industrial Conference Board, 1938.

BETTS, LILLIAN W. "Lowell, the City of Spindles," *The Outlook,* LXIX (October 12, 1901), 373–78.

Birdseye View of Lowell, Lawrence, and Other Cities. Boston: O. H. Bailey and Co., 1876.

Blue Book of the Shoe and Leather Industries. 1936–37 ed. Chicago: Hide and·Leather Publishing Co., 1936.

Boston Herald, March 7, 1937.

BROWN, R. M. "Cotton Manufacturing, North and South," *Economic Geography,* IV (January, 1928), 74–87.

BURGY, J. H. *The New England Cotton Textile Industry: A Study in Industrial Geography.* Baltimore: The Waverly Press, Inc., 1932.

COBURN, F. W. *History of Lowell and Its People.* Vol. I. New York: Lewis Historical Publishing Co., 1920.

Commonwealth of Massachusetts. *The Decennial Census, 1935.*

——, Bureau of Statistics of Labor. *The Census of Massachusetts,* 1875, 1895, 1905.

——, Bureau of Statistics. *Annual Report on the Statistics of Manufactures,* 1907–1921. Issued before 1909 by Bureau of Statistics of Labor; 1919–21 by Department of Labor and Industries.

——, Department of Labor and Industries, Division of Statistics. "Census of Manufactures in Massachusetts, Summary by Industries," 1931–36; "Census of Manufactures," 1931–36: "City of Lowell"; City of Fall River"; "City of New Bedford"; "City of Haverhill"; "Cities in Massachusetts." Mimeographed reports issued annually and separately for each city of the Commonwealth and for the Commonwealth as a whole. These reports replace the *Annual Report on the Statistics of Manufactures* after 1921.

——, Department of Labor and Industries. *Annual Report on the Statistics of Labor,* 1922–34.

——, Harbor and Land Commission. *Atlas of the Boundaries of the City of Lowell and the Towns of Ayer, Billerica, Carlisle, Chelmsford, Dracut, Dunstable,* etc. 1907.

——, *Report of the Commission on Waterways and Public Lands on the Water Resources of Massachusetts.* Senate, No. 289. Boston, 1918.

COPELAND, M. T. *The Cotton Manufacturing Industry of the United States.* Harvard Economic Studies VIII. Cambridge: Harvard University Press, 1912.

Courier Citizen Company. *Illustrated History of Lowell.* Lowell, 1897.

COWLEY, CHARLES. "Foreign Colonies in Lowell," *Old Residents Historical Association of Lowell, Contributions,* II, 165–79.

——, *A Handbook of Business in Lowell, with a History of the City.* Lowell: E. D. Green, 1856.

COWLEY, CHARLES. *Illustrated History of Lowell.* Boston: Lee and Shephard, 1868.

DAME, L. L. "The Middlesex Canal," *Old Residents Historical Association of Lowell, Contributions,* III, 272–90.

DRAKE, S. A. *History of Middlesex County.* 2 vols. Boston: Estes and Lauriat, 1880.

FAY, SAMUEL. "Carpet Weaving and the Lowell Manufacturing Company," *Old Residents Historical Association of Lowell, Contributions,* I, 52–61.

FLOYD, BENJAMIN. *The Lowell Directory, 1834.* Lowell: The Observer Press, 1834.

Form of Lease of Water Power at Lowell. (No publisher or date given. Received at Boston Public Library, 1889.)

FRENCH, J. B. "William Livingstone," *Old Residents Historical Association of Lowell, Contributions,* I, 98–104.

—— "Early Recollections of an Old Resident," *Old Residents Historical Association of Lowell, Contributions,* I, 252–61.

GERISH, E. P. *Commercial Structure of New England.* United States Department of Commerce, Domestic Commerce Series, No. 26. Washington: Government Printing Office, 1929.

GILMAN, A. "Moses Hale, an Early Manufacturer of Wool," *Old Residents Historical Association of Lowell, Contributions,* I, 243–48.

GRIFFIN, SARA S. *Quaint Bits of Lowell History.* Lowell: Butterfield Co., 1913.

HADLEY, S. P. and HILL, MABEL. "Lowell, A Character Sketch of the City," *New England Magazine,* New Series, XIX (January, 1899), 625–46.

HAMMOND, J. W. "Twentieth Century Manufactures," *Commonwealth History of Massachusetts.* Edited by A. B. Hart. Vol. V. New York: The States History Co., 1930. Pp. 370–98.

Handbook for the Visitor to Lowell. Lowell: A. Watson, 1848.

HILL, FRANK P. *Lowell Illustrated.* A Chronological Record of Events and Historical Sketches of Large Manufacturing Corporations. Lowell: Huse, Goodwin and Co., 1884.

HOPKINS, A. T. "The Old Middlesex Canal," *New England Magazine,* New Series, XVII (January, 1898), 519–32.

HOPKINS, G. M. *City Atlas of Lowell, Massachusetts.* Philadelphia, 1879.

KEIR, ROBERT MALCOLM. *Manufacturing.* New York: Ronald Press Co., 1928.

KENGOTT, G. F. *The Record of a City.* A Social Survey of Lowell, Massachusetts. New York: The Macmillan Co., 1912.

LEMERT, B. F. *The Cotton Textile Industry of the Southern Appalachian Piedmont.* Chapel Hill: University of North Carolina Press, 1933.

"Lowell and Its Manufactures," *The Merchants Magazine and Commercial Review,* XVI (April, 1847), 356–62.

Lowell Board of Trade. *Digest of the City of Lowell and Its Surrounding Towns.* Lowell, 1916.

Lowell Courier Citizen, Lowell Centennial Edition, June 30, 1936.

Lowell Directory (Annual), 1920–38. Boston, Sampson and Murdock Co.

McFALL, ROBERT J. *The External Trade of New England.* U. S. Department of Commerce, Domestic Commerce Series, No. 22. Washington: Government Printing Office, 1928.

MANN, M. W. "The Middlesex Canal, an Eighteenth Century Enterprise," *Boston Society Publications,* Vol. VI. Boston, 1910. Pp. 67–88.

MATHER, BENJAMIN. *Plan of the Town of Lowell and Belvidere Village, 1832* (map).

MEADER, J. W. *The Merrimack River.* Boston: B. B. Russel, 1869.

MILES, H. A. *Lowell as It Was and as It Is.* Lowell, 1845.

MONTGOMERY, JAMES. *A Practical Detail of the Cotton Manufacture of the United States of America and the State of Cotton Manufacture of That Country, Contrasted and Compared with That of Great Britain.* Glasgow: J. Niven, 1840.

National Industrial Conference Board. *Hours of Work as Related to Output and Health of Workers, Cotton Manufacturing.* Research Report No. 4. March, 1918.

Official American Textile Directory, 1912–37 (Annual). *Textile World* Publications. New York: McGraw-Hill Publishing Co., Inc. Published 1912–15 by Lord and Nagle Co., 1916–28 by Bragdon, Lord and Nagle.

Official Statistics of Textile Corporations. American Wool and Cotton Reporter, January 20, 1938, Section 2.

Old Residents Historicial Association of Lowell, Contributions. 6 vols. Lowell, 1874–1904.

PASQUET, D. "L'industrie du coton dans le Sud-Est des Etats-Unis," *Annales de Géographie,* XXXVIII (1929), 366–83.

Property Atlas of the City of Lowell. Philadelphia: Franklin Survey Co., 1936.

Report of the Federal Trade Commission on the Textile Industries. Part II, The Cotton Textile Industry. Washington: Government Printing Office, 1935.

SIDNEY and NEFF. *Plan of the City of Lowell in 1850* (map).

STONE, O. L. *History of Massachusetts Industries: Their Inception, Growth, and Success.* Vols. I, II. Chicago: S. J. Clarke Publishing Co., 1930.

SULLIVAN, J. L. *Remarks on the Importance of Inland Navigation from Boston by Way of the Middlesex Canal and Merrimack River in the Present and Probable Future State of Foreign Commerce.* Boston: J. Eliot, 1813.

U. S. Bureau of the Census. *Biennial Census of Manufactures, 1931.* Washington: Government Printing Office, 1935; *1923.* Washington: Government Printing Office, 1926.

U. S. Bureau of the Census. *Cotton Production and Distribution, Season of 1927–28.* Bulletin No. 164. Washington: Government Printing Office, 1928.

——. *Fifteenth Census of the United States: 1930. Population,* Vol. II; *Manufactures, 1929,* Vol. II. Washington: Government Printing Office, 1933.

——. *Fourteenth Census of the United States: 1920.* Vol. IX, *Manufactures, 1919. Reports by States, with Statistics for Principal Cities.* Washington: Government Printing Office, 1923.

——. *Location of Manufactures, 1899–1929.* Washington: Government Printing Office, 1933.

——. *Thirteenth Census of the United States: 1910.* Vol. IX, *Manufactures, 1909. Reports by States with Statistics for Principal Cities.* Washington: Government Printing Office, 1912.

U. S. Bureau of Labor Statistics. *History of Wages in the United States from Colonial Times to 1928, with Supplement, 1929–33.* Bulletin No. 604. Washington: Government Printing Office, 1934.

——. *Wages and Hours of Labor in the Boot and Shoe Industry, 1910–32.* Bulletin No. 579. Washington: Government Printing Office, 1933.

——. *Wages and Hours of Labor in Cotton Goods Manufacturing, 1924.* Bulletin No. 371. Washington: Government Printing Office, 1925.

——. *Wages and Hours of Labor in Woolen and Worsted Goods Manufacturing, 1932.* Bulletin No. 584. Washington: Government Printing Office, 1933.

U. S. Census Office. *Eleventh Census of the United States: 1890.* Vol. I, *Population,* Part I; Vol. VI, *Manufacturing Industries,* Part II. Washington: Government Printing Office, 1895.

——. *Ninth Census of the United States: 1870.* Vol. I, *Population.* Washington: Government Printing Office, 1872.

——. *Tenth Census of the United States: 1880.* Vol. II,

Manufactures. Washington: Government Printing Office, 1883; Vol. XVI. Washington: Government Printing Office, 1885.

U. S. Census Office. *Twelfth Census of the United States: 1900.* Vol. I, *Population,* Part I. Washington: U. S. Census Office, 1901.

U. S. Department of Commerce. *Statistical Abstract of the United States, 1937.* Washington: Government Printing Office, 1938.

U. S. Geological Survey. *Water Supply and Irrigation Paper 79.* Washington: Government Printing Office, 1903.

——. *Water Supply and Irrigation Paper 415.* Washington: Government Printing Office, 1916.

VANCE, R. B. *Human Geography of the South.* Chapel Hill: University of North Carolina Press, 1932.

WRIGHT, A. B. "Lowell in 1826," *Old Residents Historical Association of Lowell, Contributions,* III, 402–34.